Writing to Recover:
The Journey from Loss and Grief to a New Life

By Harriet Hodgson, BS, MA

Writing to Recover:
The Journey from Loss and Grief to a New Life

By Harriet Hodgson, BS, MA

Cover Design by Jay Highum, Rochester, Minnesota

Inside layout by Janet Sieff, Centering Corporation

The information in this book is not intended to serve as a replacement for professional advice. Any use of the information is this book is at the reader's discretion. The author and publisher specifically disclaim any and all liability arising directly or indirectly from the use or application of any information contained in this book. A medical and/or grief professional should be consulted regarding a specific situation.

Additional copies may be ordered from:
Centering Corporation – PO BOX 4600 Omaha, NE 68104
Phone: 402-553-1200 / Fax: 402-553-0507 email: centeringcorp@aol.com

1-866-218-0101

CENTERING CORPORATION
AND
GRIEF DIGEST MAGAZINE
GRIEF RESOURCES

Website: www.centering.org

Dedication

This book is for my family:

*My ancestors, who had the courage to come to America
and forge a new life;*

*My present family, loved ones who tugged me out of the darkness
into the light;*

*My future family, people I will never know,
but love anyway.*

Contents

Foreword

Perhaps because of the long history of the human race, with all its scourges, floods, and unending bloodshed, we human beings seem to have acquired a certain resilience to brace us for the disasters that occasionally befall us. And it's that resilience that enables us to live day by day with optimism for the future even though we all know that we are mortal and that tragedy is forever lurking in the form of a car accident, house fire, or unexpected terminal illness. Yet when disaster strikes, that resilience may be hard to find.

Harriet Hodgson, a professional writer and wife of a physician, knows about disaster. Does she ever! In this remarkable book she not only tells us about four successive deaths in her own family – in the space of nine months – but uses the writing of this book to express her grief by teaching potential writers like you how you can express your own grief – even if it has come as quickly and cruelly as it has to her. She even suggests her task is something like writing ***Multiple Losses for Dummies.***

Writing a book to recover from grief? It's not such a radical idea; I have known a number of grieving people who have tried to write about their losses, partly to honor the lives of those who have died and partly to help others find their way through their own grief. In fact, many books now in print were written for just those reasons. I myself am in a career that began with the terminal illness and death of my first husband, and I, too, attempted to write about it in the days following his death. When I did start serious writing 15 years later with the encouragement of my second husband, many of those ideas finally made their way into print.

Apart from the writing and editing advice, what I especially like about Harriet's book is its organization – first of all, finding your writing place, followed by writing tips to get you started, a section on writing and personal growth, what she calls "readings" or short essays, a list of proactive steps, and ending with words of hope. Unlike reading a novel or textbook, you don't have to start at the beginning and make your way page by page. You can go to the table of contents, spot readings that relate to your own grief, and start your reading right there.

What she has to offer in those readings is often practical advice that grieving people need to make their way through the worst, most painful days after a death or other loss: a mother's tool kit, setting new goals, the grief and comfort of organ donations. While circumstances and talents vary widely, she tells you what she has found helpful in her grief was returning to work immediately – in other words, writing this book! Not all grieving people will find that the answer to their grief, but aspiring writers surely will.

In the end, the resilience woven into the fabric of humanity is what ultimately must be rediscovered in every case. But it's never easy, and I'm sure that for all the grief-resolving advice Harriet has to offer here, it's hard for her too. As her brother said in his days of agony, "This is the hardest thing I've ever done in my life." And I think that applies to Harriet as well.

<hr>

Helen Fitzgerald, Emeritus Training Director of the American Hospice Foundation, author of *The Mourning Handbook, The Grieving Teen,* and *The Grieving Child*

Preface

Not knowing what life will send your way may be a good thing. If you knew the future you would worry and grieve. I had no inkling of the grief to come on Friday, February 23, 2007. On that day my daughter, Helen, died from the injuries she received in a car crash. In a desperate attempt to save her life surgeons operated on her for 20 hours. Their efforts failed because my daughter's injuries were massive and her brain activity was nil.

My twin grandchildren, who were 15 years old at the time, went into shock at their mother's death, especially my granddaughter who was also in the car. Though my granddaughter suffered a small concussion, she wasn't seriously injured, and survived the crash.

Life forced my husband and me to make painful decisions and make them quickly. We contacted the funeral home, chose a casket, purchased a burial plot, reserved the a church for the service, helped plan the service, found a photo for the program, edited the program, chose photos for a visual presentation, and sent an obituary to the newspaper. These tasks were so awful I wanted to hide under a blanket, curl up in the fetal position, and sob for days.

My former son-in-law offered to live with the twins, in the house their mother bought for them, until they graduated from high school, and we accepted his offer. The twins had enough changes to deal with and didn't need any more. Staying in their own home, surrounded by familiar things, would comfort them.

While family members were grieving for my daughter they were awaiting my father-in-law's death. Dad had gotten pneumonia and was coughing so much the Assisted Living staff sent him to the hospital by ambulance. After a week's stay in the hospital doctors realized they couldn't save Dad's life; he was too old and too ill. Dad was returned to Assisted Living and comfort care – pain-free care as life drew to a close.

Two days later, on Sunday November 25, 2007, Dad succumbed to pneumonia at 98½ years of age. Unlike my daughter's death, his death was anticipated, and the family could accept it. Dad had lived a long, productive, and meaningful life. He had lived a happy life as well. Still, it was heart-wrenching to see dad's obituary and my daughter's obituary on the same page of the newspaper.

Word of our weekend losses spread through the community with lightening speed. Phone calls started coming in, flowers were delivered daily, and we received hundreds of sympathy cards. These expressions of caring were more comforting than I anticipated. Months passed and I was doing pretty well until I received a call from my brother. He lived in Florida and, since we had been estranged for years (the reasons are unclear), I was surprised to hear from him.

"I have tongue cancer," he said, "and it has spread to my neck. I wonder if John [my physician husband] could get me into the Mayo Clinic in Jacksonville." Of course my husband agreed to help and he made some phone calls. The next day he called my brother and gave him contact information. I knew tongue cancer was difficult to treat, but thought my brother would respond to aggressive chemotherapy and survive.

"We'll visit him next month," my husband suggested, "after he is feeling better."

My brother called once more to say he was nearly finished with chemotherapy. "This is the hardest thing I've ever done in my life," he admitted. "I can hardly sit in a chair, let alone walk." We chatted briefly about other topics and then my brother said, "I love you," and hung up. Now I realize this was his goodbye.

A few weeks later, he had a heart attack and died. The memorial service and burial would be in Port Washington, Long Island. We booked a flight, reserved a hotel room, and flew to New York. My husband and I stayed only one night because we were due at a Girl Scout ceremony the next day. Our granddaughter was going to receive the Silver Award and we had promised to be there.

Losing three loved ones in five months changed my bright, happy life into a dark, bleak one. Life was grim. "I don't expect anything to go right any more," I told my husband. "All I expect is tragedy." Would I survive multiple losses? Could I be happy again? How would the losses change me? I had many questions and no answers.

One thing was certain: I had to keep writing or I would lose myself. Writing is my soul. I've been a nonfiction writer for 30 years and decided to write my way through grief. Where should I start? Usually I start with research and when I looked for resources I found technical articles, text books, first-person books, and many religious publications. Nobody had written the book I needed – *Multiple Losses for Dummies.*

Though I felt dumb, I knew I wasn't dumb, I was mourning, and decided to learn more about the process. I tracked my grief journey, identified key issues, read about them, and wrote about them. In recent years I had been writing for www.ezinearticles.com, an author's website. The site had a grief and loss category, a perfect match for my work, and I started to write articles about grief. The Internet articles would be a journal, a real-time account of my real life, and I hoped they would help others.

Writing about grief isn't a new idea. Many grief counselors ask their clients to keep a journal or diary to help them manage grief. My first article was *The Sudden Death of a Child: A Mother's Tool Kit* and I forwarded it to Helen Fitzgerald, who was, at that time, Training Director of the American Hospice Foundation. Helen had called me after I sent her a copy of my book, *Smiling Through Your Tears: Anticipating Grief,* written with Lois Krahn, MD, Chair of the Department of Psychiatry at Mayo Clinic, Scottsdale.

Since that call, Helen and I had kept in touch via email. She sent the article to the American Hospice Foundation and it was published on their website. The publication of the article made me feel good about my decision to write about grief. I began to feel hopeful about the future. Life would get better, I assured myself, and the worst was over. Friends also assured me the worst was over because "things happen in threes and you've already had three deaths."

We were wrong. Nine months later, on November 19, 2007, my former son-in-law and father of my twin grandchildren, died from injuries he received in a car crash. The circumstances surrounding his death made it doubly tragic. Apparently the highway department switched the stop signs at a busy intersection and publicized the fact in a local newspaper only. Cars that used to stop were to proceed and cars that used to proceed were to stop. The other driver didn't see the stop sign and hit my former son-in-law's car broadside.

The *Post-Bulletin* newspaper in Rochester, MN published an article about the intersection, *Death Prompts Intersection Change.* A town councilman was quoted in the article as saying there was "no chance for anybody to be safe" after the stop signs were switched. Sadly, a fourth death in the family proved his point. Katie dog, the family's beloved cocker spaniel, was injured so badly in the crash a veterinarian put her down.

"It would have been cruel to let her live," he told me later.

I couldn't believe my daughter and former son-in-law died the same way. Family members were equally stunned. "What is God thinking?" a cousin asked. Friends asked the same question. Other friends questioned God's plans for me. One friend went so far as to say God had made a mistake.

The reality of the fourth death hit me after the twins moved in with us. For years, our daughter and the twins had been coming for Sunday dinner. After dinner one night, she told us she had made a will "and you're listed as the twin's guardians. Is that okay with you?"

"Sure," we replied, dismissing the idea of her early death. Our daughter wasn't going to die. She was young, a loving mother, vibrant, productive, and moving forward in her career. The best years of her life were yet to come. I refused to think about her death on a lovely summer evening.

Now she was gone, we were the twin's guardians, and parenting teens at 72 years of age. "No offense grandma," my granddaughter said, "but living with you and grandpa will be weird." I agreed. Weird as the arrangement seemed, the four of us could still be a family, and take care of one another. I had parented teens before and would gladly do it again.

But the stresses of multiple losses took their toll. One death was devastating and multiple deaths were more so. My grief was magnified fourfold. To make things worse, I was swamped with financial and legal paperwork. I knew multiple losses would make my grief journey longer, but how much longer? The four deaths could also have unforeseen effects. In the meantime, just getting through a day was hard.

"Grief has made me stupid," I told my husband. "I can't think any more."

Stress made me clumsy and I had lots of bruises because I kept bumping into furniture and walls. In one day, alone, I hit my head four times. Odd things happened, too, like the day I filled up my car at the Pump and Munch station. Just as I was about to pull away from the pump the ignition key slipped from my hand. From the sound of the clink I thought the key landed under the front passenger seat. But when I looked under the front seat I couldn't find it. As the two station employees watched from the window, I crawled around on the pavement, with my butt in the air, and looked under all of the car seats. No key.

I went into the station, explained my problem, asked to use the phone, and called my husband. By now I was crying and the station employees were looking at me worriedly. "Life has been hard lately," I blubbered. "Four of my family members have died."

"Don't worry," one man said. "I'll find your key." Despite the cold temperature, he followed me to the car in his shirtsleeves, looked under all the seats, and couldn't find the key. Then he felt the small floor depressions under the driver's seat and found it. He handed the key to me and grinned.

Tears drizzled down my face and I could hardly speak. "Thank you for your kindness," I said. The man put his arms around me, patted my back, and told me to "take care." Life really was out of control. A stranger was hugging me, I was hugging him and, at the rate we were going, we would be sending each other greeting cards.

I was able to smile about the incident later and it taught me an important lesson. Bad things happen to good people and when they do, good people – even strangers – reach out to help. The thought comforted me and I held it close to my heart.

Grief is universal, something people of all races, cultures, and religions experience. Knowing that I wasn't alone in my grief was reassuring, but I was still overwhelmed with grief, and couldn't stop crying. I described my feelings in an article, ***Another Death – How Much Can a Family Take?*** I emailed the article to Helen Fitzgerald. She thought the article was excellent, "but so sad," and suggested compiling all of the articles into an anthology.

The idea surprised me. How could I, a professional writer, not know I was writing a book? Though I'd printed out the articles, put them in a binder, and donated the binder to my church library, I didn't think of them as an anthology. In my mind the articles were a donation and nothing more. Go figure.

I took Helen's suggestion and wrote a book outline. But I was worried about getting mired in the raw emotions of grief, so I decided to end the book on the first anniversary of my daughter's death. Besides, I could feel the book coming to a close and that was a good thing – a sign of recovery. Writing had gotten me through a challenging year.

During that year I learned more than I wanted to know about grief. "Life has made you a grief expert," a marketing contact said. I never thought I would write this book, yet it's the most important one I've ever written. ***Writing to Recover*** may be an important book for you, as well, and help you see the role that writing plays in the recovery process.

There are many reasons to write about your grief. You may write to identify feelings, express anger, explore dreams, document family history, correct family history, rekindle religious beliefs, track recovery mileposts, plan a new life, and more. As the pages accumulate you will get a clearer picture of your grief journey. More important, you get a clearer picture of yourself.

Each of us recovers from loss in our own way, at our own pace, and on our own terms. Whether you're grieving for one loss or many, I hope you sit down and write. Like me, you may find you're not only writing to recover, you're writing to survive. Writing your way through grief helps you find your way through grief. And that is a blessing.

Using This Book

This book has one purpose – to get you to write about your grief. The articles, or readings as they are called in the contents, will give you some writing ideas. While you're reading the articles look for the action steps I took to feel better. Think about the action steps you've already taken and the ones you may take in the days ahead.

With a few exceptions, the first versions of the articles appeared on www.ezinearticles.com and they are copyright in my name. I revised the articles to make them fit together and correct some English errors. When I saw the errors I was embarrassed. A professional writer shouldn't be making silly mistakes like forgetting the letter s to indicate a plural. Then I cut myself some slack. My writing came from the depths of anguish. Who thinks about correct English at a time like that? Not me, and I would venture to say, not you.

The last article, **Remembering Your Loved One with a Memory Cook Book**, was actually the first in the **Writing to Recover** series. I wrote it after my mother-in-law died and included it in the anthology because it's an example of making something good from grief. The article also ends the book on a happy note.

As a non-fiction writer, I'm used to citing sources to support the points I make. You will find a list of reliable resources at the back of the book. At this stressful time you don't need an encyclopedia; you need reliable information and you need it fast. So I've kept the readings short and the average length is 500 words. While the readings are published in chronological order, you don't have to read them that way. Scan the titles and choose the ones you want to read first.

World religions have much to teach us and I have learned from them. I want this anthology to appeal to readers of all faiths and so, while I cite religious experts, I do not promote any specific religion. In case you're wondering, I belong to a church and received support from my church community during my grief journey. Writing this book has been a religious and spiritual experience for me.

Because it is hard to keep track of your thoughts when you're grieving, I've added notes pages to the book. Use these pages to jot down your feelings, your writing ideas, the names of grief organizations and websites, contact information, "To Do" lists, or even your grocery list. The pages may also be used for doodling if you're a doodling kind of person.

Please make this book your own. Underline important points, write notes in the margins, and fold down corners of the pages. The grief journey is a confusing and stressful one. You may become so stressed you don't want to read or can't remember what you read. If this happens, put the book down for a while and give your mind a rest.

Return to the book again when you're feeling better. Some parts may be worth a second read, especially the section, Writing Tips for You, and four articles:

- Why I Am Writing About my Grief
- Writing Your Way Through Grief
- Grieving and Gratefulness for a Writing Career
- Seting New Goals After a Loved One Has Died

Losing a loved one is terribly painful, and the pain of multiple losses is almost beyond words. I can't take your pain away, but I can offer you these words of comfort: You will get though this awful time. Others have survived tragedy and you will, too. Grief will change your life and you will always miss your loved ones. Still, life is a miracle. Live it for your loved ones and yourself.

Your Writing Place

Where you write influences what you write. Thirty years ago, when I first started writing, I wrote in the basement on an electric typewriter and a rickety typewriter table next to the utility room. It was a noisy room and I could hear the hot water heater turn on, the hum of the furnace and, in the summer months, the hum of the air conditioner.

All of these sounds were distractions. Learning how to ignore these distractions took me years and, today, I can write almost anywhere. I have also invested in better equipment: a computer, computer chair, work station, printer, and fax machine.

You may be used to writing if you keep a diary or journal. However, if you're new to writing you need to stack the odds in your favor. To do this you need two things – a place to think and a place to write. These things may be in different areas, on different levels, or outdoors, where you can be close to nature.

Your thinking place should be a quiet place, away from the hustle and bustle of life. Look around your home now and find a comfortable chair or couch. To see if you're really comfortable, sit there for a while and let your mind wander. Do this for several days. Change your thinking place if it makes you uncomfortable.

My thinking place was the family room couch and I sat there for days. The television was on and the sound was off. I tuned the set to the home and garden channel and looked at the screen occasionally to give my mind a break from grief. A stranger would have thought I was mentally ill and had "gone over the edge." But I knew writing began with thinking.

I thought about the gaping holes death had cut from my life. I thought about happy relationships and sad ones. I thought about regrets and anger and despair. I thought about the power of love. These thoughts were my writing homework. Then I went downstairs to the office and expressed my grief in words. Your writing preparation may be similar to mine.

Once you have your thinking place it's time to find your writing place. If you write at a computer make sure the chair is adjusted properly. You also need adequate lighting. Many experts think the light source should come from the left, but overhead lighting works just as well. I have overhead lighting and an extra lamp for gray days and nighttime work.

Writers, including beginning ones, usually have a beverage near by, coffee, tea, juice, or water. More than once, I've rested my coffee cup on a pile of books and spilled coffee all over my notes. So rest your cup or glass on a level spot, well away from the computer. Friends of mind have ruined their computer keyboards by spilling drinks on them.

You will need storage space in addition to writing and thinking space. Keep your writing in an office file cabinet, portable file holder, or a box with a lid. Share your writing with loved ones and friends if you wish.

Writing about your grief doesn't mean you can't express your grief artistically – painting, quilting, sketching, sculpture, singing, composing, and more. Vamik D. Volkan, MD and Elizabeth Zintl, authors of **Life After Loss: The Lessons of Grief,** think of artistic expressions as "unconscious negotiations." According to them, poetic elegy is the most obvious example of unconscious negotiations. "Others of us, less artistically inclined, assemble a scrapbook, [or] organize a photo collage," they say. "In our deliberation over what to include, we are doing the work of mourning."

Writing Tips for You

Some dictionaries define diary and journal with the same words. While these writing forms are similar, they are also quite different. Christina Baldwin, author of **One to One: Self-Understanding Through Journal Writing**, defines a diary as a formal pattern of daily entries that document your activities, experiences, and observations.

Daily is the key word here and it's also the problem. With multiple losses there is little time, if any, to write in a diary every day. You may, however, find the time to write occasional entries in a journal.

According to Baldwin, a journal is a more casual form of writing than a diary. She defines it as an "intermittent record of an inner life, written consistently, but not on a daily basis." Baldwin thinks a journal is just the place to tuck away snippets of your daily life. "We discover this naturally by what we learn to put in writing, and by what we include in addition to writing," she explains.

Psychotherapist Kathleen Adams, of the Center for Journal Therapy, describes the journal writing process in her website article, **Managing Grief Through Journal Writing.** Adams thinks most people "will open themselves up and pour themselves out onto the [journal] page." That's why I encourage you to write about your grief.

Open yourself up, pour yourself out, and discover yourself in the words you write. You may also pour out your feelings in articles, poems, books, and talks. I write on a computer because it saves time, revisions are easy, and printing is fast. If you don't have a computer (and some people don't) you may use a tape recorder. You may also write on an old-fashioned typewriter or in longhand.

Grief counselor Bob Deits, MTh offers tips for journal writing in his book, *Life After Loss: A Practical Guide to Renewing Your Life After Experiencing Major Loss.* He thinks a stenographer's notebook works well for journal and diary writing. Deits tells readers to write the date and time of their entries at the top of the page. As for things to write about, Deits thinks readers may write about significant events, important people, life changes and plans for tomorrow.

Many people are intimidated by writing and you may be one of them. Still, your thoughts and ideas are worth putting into words. These writing tips worked for me and I think they will work for you. You may think of other tips as you're writing and, if you do, please add them to the list.

• Give yourself enough thinking time.

• Become aware of your thoughts, even the ones that fly by like birds.

• Carry a small pad with you and jot down your stream of consciousness thoughts.

• Put your thoughts into words as quickly as you can.

• Try and write for 15 minutes a day.

• Don't worry about spelling, grammar or punctuation.

• Be honest with your feelings even if they are scary.

• Name your feelings if you can. If you can't, that's OK.

• If you get stuck, put your writing aside for a while.

• If you get really stuck jot down a word or two.

• Use your journal for "To Do" lists if you wish. Cross off the items as you do them.

• Write about your wishes for the future.

• Read your work aloud to get a sense of word flow.

• Keep on writing.

Writing and Personal Growth

If you keep at it, writing about grief leads to personal growth. Writing also increases your emotional intelligence, a term coined by Daniel Goleman, PhD, author of **Working With Emotional Intelligence**. Unlike IQ, which diminishes slowly over time, Goleman says emotional intelligence may increase throughout life. Perhaps you have seen signs of this increase already.

Becoming aware of personal growth is rather like fog lifting on a gray morning. At first, you see only fuzzy shapes. As the fog dissipates you start to see details. Finally, you are able to see clear images – your personal growth. What kinds of changes might you expect? These examples are from my life. Your personal growth may be similar to mine or quite different.

You may be aware of new issues. Before I wrote anything, I followed my stream of consciousness thoughts. Issues flashed through my mind and I put them in categories: unimportant, pretty important, and very important. Unimportant stuff was discarded and I learned more about the very important. I'm a self-aware person, but some key issues, such as probate, staying busy, and anniversary reactions, came as a surprise.

Anger may be an issue for you. In her article, **10 Grief Steps,** posted on the Sound Feelings website, poet Roe Ziccarello describes the anger she felt after the death of her son. She kept a grief journal and, despite shock, depression and emotional numbness, continued to make entries.

Later, when she read her journal, Ziccarello says her anger, blame and pain almost jumped off the page and grabbed her by the throat. She was able to harness her pain and says, "Chronicling the journey has allowed me to assess my own grief work." You may use your writing to assess your grief work. What have you done so far? What needs to be done?

You may be a more sensitive person. Sensitivity is more than a learned skill; it's a hard-earned skill, according to Vamik D. Volkan, MD and Elizabeth Zintl, authors of *Life After Loss: The Lessons of Grief.* They describe the lessons of grief as "brutal gifts" that lead to new maturity and self-understanding. Before my losses, I was a sensitive person and I am even more sensitive now.

My emotional radar is always on and I can sense people who are in emotional pain. You may do this, too. Bereaved people – you and I – need to talk about their departed loved ones and the pain of loss. Your writing will reveal your sensitivity. In time, you will be able to apply this sensitivity to life.

Everything you say and do reveals your "listening soul." Bettyclare Moffatt describes the listening soul in her book, *Soulwork*. When you learn to be still, to listen to your own soul, you become a center of light, Moffatt says, and "you can illuminate any relationship, any situation, with this light."

You may change your idea of what's important. Isn't it funny how life works? You get caught up in trivial things and then grief changes everything. Unimportant things fall away like chaff from wheat. The dictionary defines chaff as husks of grains and grasses separated during threshing. Chaff becomes animal fodder or rubbish. During my grief journey I learned to distinguish important stuff from rubbish. Writing helped me to make this distinction and it may also help you.

As I walk along the recovery road, however, I have found that I have to give myself occasional tune-ups. When I feel rushed or anxious I ask myself, "Is this really important?" Answering this question helps me to avoid detours and gets me back on the recovery road. The important things have been reduced to a precious few. I work on them all the time.

You may be more forgiving. Rabbi Harold Kushner discusses forgiveness in his book, **When Bad Things Happen to Good People.** After bad things happen, Kushner says we are left with anguish and a sense of unfairness. He asks if we can forgive the imperfect people who have hurt us and a God that permits bad luck, sickness and cruelty. If we are able do to this, Kushner adds, we will "recognize that the ability to forgive and the ability to love are the weapons God has given us to enable us to live fully, bravely, and meaningfully... ."

The ability to forgive adds new meaning to our lives. While you are in the forgiving mode, you may as well forgive yourself for not being perfect. There is no perfect way to grieve, express sorrow, or recover from loss. You do the best you can, or as friends have told me, "You just keep putting one foot in front of the other."

You may turn or return to your faith. When a loved one dies it's normal to turn to religion and spirituality for support. Faith can help you heal from tragedy, according to Dr. Robert Veniga, author of **A Gift of Hope: How We Survive Our Tragedies.** When tragedy strikes we want to run away, Veniga explains and, since there is no place to run, we may turn to faith.

"Faith has a powerful effect in helping people recover a sense of balance, tranquility and hope," writes Veniga.

Writing about your grief may become a search for answers. Your religious and spiritual beliefs may stay the same, shift a bit, or change. Grief strengthened my beliefs and I try to live them daily. My grief writing covered many topics. You may choose to write only about your faith and that is a personal decision.

You may savor the miracle of life. While I understand the miracle of life, I understand it better after reading Heather Lende's book, **If You Lived Here, I'd Know Your Name.** Lende lives in Alaska and writes obituaries for the **Chilkat Valley News.** Her book is real, stark, beautiful, funny and touching. At the end of the book Lende tells a story about the death of her beloved dog, Carl.

Good Dog Carl, as she calls him, taught the family a lesson about life and death. His death reminded her that we come from dust and return to dust. Lende hasn't resigned herself to this reality of life, indeed, she doesn't approve. Still, she knows what it means to be a wife, mother and writer in Haines, Alaska. "This is my life, and I am grateful," she says.

I read this line again and again. Every time I read it I cried. "I am grateful" became a mantra for my grief journey.

Gratefulness has given new purpose to my life. While I don't know how long I will live, I know there is more living to be done. This is the greatest lesson of my grief and it may be the greatest lesson of yours. Writing from the heart takes courage. The more you write the more courage you have. And the more courage you have the more beautiful life becomes.

Reading 1

<hr/>

The Sudden Death of a Child: A Mother's Tool Kit

Two deaths in one weekend have been overwhelming. I can't focus my thoughts and I keep losing things. These grief responses are bad enough, but I've also become a physical klutz. Grief has made me Mrs. Bumbly Stumbly.

Fortunately, I'm a health writer and have written about grief. This helps me to see where I am in the grief process and I've taken steps to cope with my grief. Right now there are six items in my tool kit, and I may add others. My coping tools may help you cope with the death of a child and here they are.

Let yourself cry. In his book, *The Language of Tears*, Jeffrey A. Kottler says we need to give ourselves permission to cry. I did this and decided I would cry any time, anywhere, for as long as needed. Though I still burst into tears, my sobbing has stopped. Crying has really helped me.

Find comfort in friends. Each phone call, each email, each card is a candle in the darkness. Two friends came to the house and enfolded me in their arms. Another friend called and talked about the loss of her brother at age 20. When I told her my husband and I have assured our twin grandchildren of a college education she said, "That's good. You have planted goals in their minds."

Find comfort in tasks. Ordinary things – laundry, dishes, grocery shopping, cleaning – have been comforting. I don't know why, but doing these things gives my grief a rest. Daily tasks also give my life the structure it needs.

Do your job. Well-meaning friends have told me to take a break from writing. I have not followed their advice, for if I do, I have not only lost family members, I have lost my identity. My husband is a retired physician and he has returned to work part-time. I am back on my daily writing schedule.

Get help if you need it. I decided to seek help anywhere I could and to accept this help. Though we have only met via email, I contacted Helen Fitzgerald, Emeritus Training Director of the American Hospice Foundation. She printed *Remembering You* booklets from the foundation website for our grandkids and also sent me a copy of her book, *The Grieving Teen*. The church has also offered to provide grief counseling for our grandchildren.

See the spirit. When a child dies many people don't know what to say. For me, the most comforting words have been, "I'm so sorry." Some people have made comments that reflect spiritual beliefs different from mine. I accepted these comments in the caring spirit in which they were given.

My husband and I don't believe in "closure." Though we will learn to live with our daughter's sudden death, there will always be a hole in our lives. We will honor our daughter's life by living each day to the fullest and loving the grandchildren she gave us.

Reading 2

Finding Hope After the Death of a Child

The shock of my daughter's death is still with me. It will be with me forever, not as intense, but always there. Fortunately, I am blessed to have twin grandchildren and my new mission in life is caring for them. My husband and I share this mission.

I know my grandchildren and they know me. They know I love them, will care for them, and keep my promises. Though they are living with their father, my mind is filled with parenting thoughts about them. Do you have lunch money? Has your bus fee been paid? What clothes do you need?

Somehow, while I am dealing with questions, legal procedures and financial ones, I must find hope. It's not easy. Every day I look for hope, for as a health writer, I know its spark can keep me going. Where is my hope?

My daughter was an organ donor. After consulting with our grandchildren, my husband and I signed an agreement with Life Source to donate our daughter's organs. The Life Source representative called the next day. "Your daughter saved three lives," she said, "and because of her, another will see." Knowing my daughter helped others gives me hope.

Friends have showered us with kindness. Because my husband and I are active in the community we have received cards from friends, people we barely know, and strangers. Some of the comments on the cards make us cry, yet we are comforted by them. The kindness of others gives me hope.

Memorials in my daughter's name give me hope. At the end of our daughter's obituary we suggested memorials to Mayo Clinic. The memorials we have received add up to a substantial donation to Mayo. Helping Mayo Clinic to carry out its mission of medical practice, education, and research gives me hope.

My daughter imprinted her values on her children. The twins started thinking about their mother's values the moment she died. "Even when Mom disciplined us she was never angry," my grandson said. "Mommy always made people smile," my granddaughter said. The twins know their mother wanted them to go to college and we will make this dream come true – a mission that gives us hope.

The signs of spring lift my spirits. The piles of snow around the house are melting and I am starting to see green grass. Next to the house, the birch trees show signs of budding. I saw my first robin yesterday. She (or he) sat on a tree near the house and sang for several minutes. Spring gives me hope and I am looking forward to it.

These hopeful signs are helping to heal my grief. I am trying to make something good from grief and writing articles is one way to do this. Grief is a common bond that joins people together and makes us human.

Reading 3

Delivering Food to a Family After the Death of a Loved One

I've delivered food to grieving families and you probably have, too. Once I delivered a large casserole of beef stew with burgundy, something I wouldn't do now. After having two family members die on the same weekend, I have a different slant on food deliveries. Food is appreciated, but I think we need to update the custom, and here are my suggestions.

Call first. You don't know how much food has already been delivered. The refrigerator and freezer may be full and additional food will cause problems. Before you make anything call and see if the family needs food. When a church friend called I turned down her offer of food. "It's all we can do to eat a scrambled egg," I explained.

Consider portion sizes. Some family members appreciate large food deliveries, but others are overwhelmed by them. Dividing food into small portions encourages family members to eat. Packaging food in small freezer containers is also helpful.

Offer to shop. Going to the grocery store after my daughter's death took all the courage I had. I would meet friends at the store and burst into tears when they expressed sympathy. Offer to pick up some groceries for the family the next time you shop. Tell them when you will deliver the groceries.

Check back later. The family is overwhelmed with legal and financial tasks after the death of a loved one. They may run out of milk or basic supplies like toilet paper. Contact the family again and see if they need anything.

No thanks are necessary. Years ago, when our family was in crisis, a church friend gave me some soup. A note was taped to the top of the bowl and it read, "No thanks are necessary. I wanted to do this for you." This is a stressful time for all family members. Telling them that no thanks are necessary helps to relieve their stress.

Delivering food is a time-honored custom and one worthy of continuing. The best food you can provide is food for the soul and the words, "I'm so sorry."

Reading 4

Setting New Goals After a Loved One Has Died

I know things will never be the same, yet I have to live my life. How do I go about it? Pesach Krauss and Morrie Goldfisher write about getting on with life in their book, *Why Me? Coping with Grief, Loss and Change.*

After a loved one dies Krauss and Goldfisher think we need to shift our focus from a direct relationship with the deceased to identifying with his or her values. "In that way, we free ourselves from the cold grip of the past to embrace warm and tender memories and action for the present," they write.

I'm blessed to have many warm and tender memories of my father-in-law and daughter. The family values of hard work, honesty, education, and giving back have been passed from one generation to the next – another blessing. But I'm so overwhelmed by grief I fear I will get stuck in the past. I didn't want this to happen and started to think about new goals.

Daniel Goleman, author of *Emotional Intelligence,* thinks people who pursue their goals have less anxiety and stress. Though the last few weeks have been filled with distress, I thought I could identify new goals. One goal was already clear. The instant our daughter died, my husband and I dedicated ourselves to protecting and caring for our grandchildren. "There must be other goals," I muttered to myself.

And so, while I was making the bed, washing dishes, and folding laundry, I let my mind wander. This went on for several weeks. Suddenly, the fog lifted from my mind and I saw my new goals clearly. I think they are good ones.

Goal 1: I will be a role model for my grandchildren.

Goal 2: I will tell them, in concise words, how I will help them.

Goal 3: I will keep my promises.

Goal 4: I will continue to write.

Goal 5: I will share my grief experiences.

Goal 6: I will learn and grow from grief.

Goal 7: I will laugh whenever I can.

Goal 8: I will care for myself so I can care for others.

Goal 9: I will cherish each day.

Goal 10: I will celebrate life with my husband and family.

Identifying new goals has given new meaning to my life. While I still have bouts of crying (sometimes in my sleep) I awaken with a sense of purpose. I have this day and will make the most of it.

Reading 5

What Can Kids Hold onto After a Parent has Died?

It has been just over a month since my daughter died. Every day has been a day of tears, some voiced, some silent. My 15-year-old twin grandchildren are so overcome with grief they're almost paralyzed. Both of them are looking for reminders of their mom, things they can hold onto, and my husband and I have given them things.

The twins want to hear stories about their mother. But it is the values she instilled in them – values passed from one generation to the next – that will help them most. So I typed a list of their mother's values for them. The title is *Some of the Values Your Mother Gave You.* Other values will become clear in time. Values are something the kids can hold into, indeed, they are a prescription for life. Here is the list.

1. Family comes first. Your mother found love and support in her family. She wanted you to have this, too, which is why we had Pampa for dinner when you came and why she took you to see him when he was dying.
2. Get an education. Read your mother's resume and you will see that she was always learning. She knew more knowledge would lead her to better jobs and a better life.
3. Work hard. Your mother worked hard for you. That is why she got up at the crack of dawn and drove two hours to her job and two hours home. She wanted you to live in the house she chose for you and attend the high school you wanted to attend.
4. Be a caring, spiritual person. Your mother believed that kindness leads to more kindness and this is why she was a Girl Scout leader, a church volunteer, and gave back to the community in other ways.
5. Share what you have. There were times in life when your mother didn't have much, but she always shared what she had: extra children's clothing, appliances, food (Christmas cookies and apple pie) and plants. Sharing made your mother feel good inside.
6. Be honest and ethical. When your mother worked for one company, a disgruntled worker threatened to take shortcuts because she was a female and his boss. His threat was not only unethical, it was unsafe, and your mother told him if he left out one bolt she would shut down production.
7. Laugh every day. Thanks to *The Big Book* (Alcoholics Anonymous) and the way she lived her life, your mother found laughter in life. Laughter energized her and delighted those around her. Your mother would want you to laugh every day and enjoy the life you have.

Reading 6

The Shock of Sudden Death and Probate

When my daughter was suddenly killed in a car crash, I was overcome with grief. She was at a secure place in life, well-educated, mature, excited about her children and her job. My father-in-law died the same weekend and, though we expected his death, it was still a shock. I am co-executor of my daughter's estate.

While I am glad she had a will, her finances are a mystery. My husband and I have become financial detectives, tracking down leads and trying to make sense of them. Grief and Probate are a heavy burden, a burden filled with questions. We must answer these questions and more.

What bank did she use? Did she have a safe-deposit box? How much cash does she have? What bills are outstanding? Did she have any stocks and bonds? Does she owe money on her two cars? Is she still owed salary? If so, can we deposit her salary? What benefits is she entitled to? What is the homestead value of her house? What is the market value? How much is her personal property worth? Did she pay her taxes?

These questions add up to a financial nightmare, and we were already living a grief nightmare. You can avoid similar circumstances by doing your financial homework. What does this homework involve?

1. Review your will. Laws may have changed and you may have to change the wording of your will or, as in our case, the executor.
2. Hire a lawyer. We needed two lawyers, one to help with our daughter's Will and Probate, and another to help with her home and personal property.
3. Put financial information in writing. Write down the name of your bank, your account number(s), the number of your safe-deposit box if you have one. Give the list to someone you trust.
4. Record investments. You may keep this record yourself, or ask your stock broker or financial advisor to do it. The important thing is to have written proof of your investments.
5. Have your home appraised. Ask a professional appraiser to determine the current value of your home and photocopy the appraisal. Put one copy in your safe-deposit box and give the other to a trusted relative.
6. Photograph possessions. These photos are legal proof of ownership. Pay attention to detail when you take the photos. For example, if you collect rare books, photograph the covers. Put the electronic chip or developed photos in your safe-deposit box.
7. Inventory your home. I have just started this process and am going to buy a software program to help me with the inventory.
8. Put special requests in writing. These requests may include family heirlooms, art work, special collections and specific items, such as a boat. Tell relatives/friends about your intentions. Again, put the list in your safe-deposit box.

In case you are wondering, I'm taking my own advice. I don't want my remaining daughter or grandchildren to go through the same financial nightmare. Doing your financial homework is a gift for those you love.

Reading 7

Why I am Writing About my Grief

My daughter's death ended my "ordinary" life and it will never be ordinary again. She is gone, her twins are without a mother, and I am without a daughter. Because I've written about grief before, I'm moving quickly through its stages. I've decided to write about my grief and for good reasons.

This is what I do. I'm a writer and have no intention of stopping. To stop would feel like another death in the family. Ironically, one of my recent books is about anticipatory grief. Sometimes writers can predict their next work and sometimes they can't. I don't know the exact topics, but I know I'll write about grief. I'll write about happy things, too, for I know happy moments are ahead.

Writing is a kind of diary. Friends who have gone through the grief process told me to keep a diary. This is good advice, but unnecessary because I've already written about grief. I've written about the grief of caring for a demented loved one, coping with grief during the holidays, and grief work people must do. All of these articles came from life experience.

I learn more. As a health writer, I must document my work. During 30 years of writing I have gathered a small library of reference books. One of the most helpful is **When Bad Things Happen to Good People** by Harold S. Kushner. For me, the main message of the book is that grieving people try to explain death when there is no explanation. My daughter's death was a tragic accident and I must accept this fact.

Learning brings understanding. Therese A. Rando, PhD, writes about the death of a child in **How to Go On Living When Someone You Love Dies.** She describes the death of a child as an unusual, out-of-turn event that threatens identity. I understand what Rando means. Clearly, I'm not the same person today as I was when my daughter died. My future hinges on a new mission of protecting my grandchildren and I will fulfill this mission.

I can help others. Parents have two choices when a child dies. One is to get stuck in grief and the other is to move forward with purpose. I've always tried to write books and articles that help people. The untimely death of my daughter has revitalized this purpose.

Judy Tatelbaum, in her book, **The Courage to Grieve,** makes a case for creating something from grief. "Making our grief meaningful can be the antidote to despair and suffering as well as a stepping-stone to personal growth and achievement," she says. That is why I'm writing about grief and walking, step by step, to tomorrow.

Reading 8

Teen Grief—A Time for Patience

Grief is difficult at any age, but it's especially difficult for teens. As www. hospice.net notes, "Teens are no longer children, yet neither are they adults." While teens are grappling with grief, they're also grappling with emotional, physical, academic and, sometimes, family pressures.

Teen responses to grief are similar to adult responses, according to the National Institute of Mental health (NIMH). As Dr. Alan Wolfelt, founder and director of the Center for Loss and Life Transition in Fort Collins, Colorado, says on the NIMH website, "The adolescent may feel extreme guilt over his or her failure to prevent the loss of life."

Teen grief became very real after my daughter was killed. Though teens learn from adults, I'm learning from my 15-year-old grandchildren. The things I've learned may help grieving teens in your family, school or church. Here they are.

- Involve teens. Teens may want to have a say in whether to bury or cremate their loved one. Asking them to help with the memorial service is another way to involve them. Months from now, teens may wish to create a memorial, such as planting a tree in memory of their loved one.
- Encourage tears. In his book, *The Language of Tears,* Jeffrey A. Kottler describes crying as a healthy and necessary human process. But teens may hold back tears and try to act strong. We can help teens by telling them it's OK to cry.
- Keep a routine. Routines are familiar and provide structure for teen lives that are out of control. More important, routines are often links to help lines – support groups, school/church counselors and caring friends.
- Tell stories. Talking about the deceased helps to keep that person alive in a teen's mind. Teens want to hear funny, uplifting stories from family members and friends. They may wish to compile these stories in a memory book.
- Use peers. Helen Fitzgerald, Emeritus Training Director of the American Hospice Foundation, thinks teens often trust peers only. A church message board may help grieving teens more than formal counseling. Many teens write about grief on blogs and this is called P 2 P communication.
- Hug cautiously. When strangers hear about a teen's loss they often hug them. Teens may see these hugs as an invasion of personal space and privacy. Before you hug a teen ask him or her for permission to do so.
- Be gentle. You need to be a good, non-judgmental listener to gain a teen's trust, according to Helen Fitzgerald. So let teens know you love them and will care for them. "Support their ideas or gently introduce new ways to approach their ideas," advises Fitzgerald.

See a future. Making plans for the future, such as going to camp, helps teens to see a future and the return of happiness. We eventually have to let go of grief, explains BettyClare Moffatt in her book, *Soulwork: Clearing the Mind, Opening the Heart, Replenishing the Spirit.* "Let tomorrow come in joy," she writes. "Begin again. Begin now."

Reading 9

My Daughter's Death and How I Am Honoring Her Life

It's been two months since my daughter died and I've cried every day. Though I know she is gone, I expect her to walk in the door at any minute and say, "Hi." I think she will call me and we will talk about weekend plans. None of this will happen. Still, I'm remembering my daughter in many ways.

1. Church library donations. A couple of years ago I co-authored a book about anticipatory grief. I donated copies of the book to my church library. In addition, I printed out the Internet articles I'd written about grief and put them on a notebook. I also donated a copy of Helen Fitzgerald's book, *The Grieving Teen*, to the library.

2. Keeping traditions. Every Sunday my daughter and the twins came for dinner. The week after her death I was so overcome with grief I couldn't fix dinner, but I asked the twins and my former son-in-law to come the next. They came and, though all of us cried, we were glad to be together. I plan to keep other traditions as well.

3. Memorial flower garden. Minnesotans have waited a long time for spring and it's finally here. As soon as bedding plants are available, the twins and I will plant a garden in memory of their mom. We may also plant a flowering tree in the back yard.

4. Carrying out plans. My daughter was in the process of finishing the lower level of her home. The kids helped plan the layout and were going to help with painting and laying the floor. After a family discussion, we decided to go ahead with the project. We're also going to put a small deck on the house because that's what their mother planned.

5. Fixing favorite foods. Both the twins (one boy, one girl) like to cook. They asked me for their mother's recipe for Swedish meat balls. I emailed the recipe to them. The twins made the meatballs and loved them. My daughter had other favorite foods, and I'll make them for my grandkids.

6. Telling stories. I come from a story-telling family. Everyone in the family knows it's important to tell stories about my daughter, and we're telling them. We tell them lovingly, laugh together and cry a bit. Stories are verbal snapshots for our grandkids and we hope they'll remember them forever.

Sticking with values. To help my grandkids cope with grief, I've talked with them about their mother's values. I typed up a list of her values and gave it to them. While they appreciated my reminder, they didn't really need it. My daughter was a marvelous mother and she made her values clear. Her kids are living them now.

Reading 10

Grief and the Miracles of Kindness

I want to be up-to-date on things, but limit the amount of television news I watch. Television news is depressing and few programs have good news stories. Kindness is rarely reported on television news. Indeed, I began to think kindness had disappeared from modern life.

After my daughter and father-in-law died, I changed my mind. I have a caregiving type of personality and, though I've done kind things for others, I was unprepared for the outpouring of kindness I received.

A church friend gave me a copy of **Thirst**, a book of poetry by Pulitzer Prize-winner Mary Oliver. Oliver's poem, **In the Storm**, changed my view of kindness. "Kindness – as now and again some rare person has suggested – is a miracle," she writes. Before I read the poem, I thought kindness was a personal value learned in childhood. Now I see kindness as a true miracle of life.

Sympathy cards were the first kindness I received. Word of our family tragedies flashed around the community like lightning. My husband and I have received hundreds of cards. One handmade card, with an original poem lettered on the front, was especially beautiful. I was touched by this example of creativity and kindness.

Flowers were another kindness, and they arrived in many forms – a single yellow rose in a bud vase, an elegant white bouquet, and vases of multi-colored flowers. Two flower deliveries stand out in my mind. One was a basket of tiny blue flowers from an organization I belong to and another was a terrarium from a neighbor. What thoughtful gifts. What kindness.

Financial memorials in memory of my daughter and father-in-law have been kindnesses, too. Memorials were suggested to Mayo Clinic. Donations from individuals and organizations have added up to a sizeable amount of money. These kindnesses have touched the core of my being.

The phone calls I have received were especially touching. I've received calls from friends in Canada, England, and all across the country. Some were so shocked by our family tragedies they cried as they spoke to me. Their empathy was real, a miracle of kindness.

Friendships have also been miracles of kindness. Two friends took me to lunch to get me out of the house. We talked about local news, global issues, our families, coping with grief, and we laughed a lot. Another friend, at least I think he was the one, left a pot of pansies on the deck. The sweet, colorful pansies made me cry.

Judy Tatelbaum, in her book, **The Courage to Grieve**, writes about help from family members and friends. "The supportive encouragement to go on with life can be an essential element in recovering from grief," according to Tatelbaum. Miracles of kindness have changed my life and are helping me to find hope again. I will pass them on some time, some day.

Reading 11

Grieving and Gratefulness for a Writing Career

Seven days after my daughter and father-in-law died, I wrote an Internet article about grief. I wrote several more articles and was starting to recover, when my brother died of cancer. Three deaths in five months felled me and I stopped writing.

But, as I discovered, life wasn't life without writing. In fact, I grieved for the lack of writing. Writing was – and is – my way of coping. Would the distractions of grief prevent me from writing? The only way to find out was to write again. I'm grateful for my writing career and its many blessings.

Writing diverts my mind. If you've had a death in the family, you know grief wears you out. As my 15-year-old grandson said, "I'm so tired of crying." Sometimes you have to take a break from grief, and writing does that for me. Instead of obsessing about tragedy, I let my mind roam free. And it does roam free as I hunt for article and book ideas. Some of the things I've written about have surprised me. Writing is a mental vacation that takes me to new and surprising places.

Writing forces me to focus. When I'm writing I have to focus on one topic. Once I'm focused I think about the points to make and their order. Though I may struggle with word retrieval and sentence flow, I'm still able to stay focused. Of course I think about my deceased loved ones when I'm writing, but it's just for a few seconds, and I return to the task at hand. The best way to honor my loved ones is to enjoy each day and what I do. I know my daughter, father-in-law, and brother would not want me to get mired in grief. Life is too precious for that.

Writing keeps language skills sharp. These skills are more than punctuation, spelling and grammar. I have to be attuned to current events, hot topics, and trends. Writers are supposed to write about what they know, and I just wrote an article about taking a tree down in our yard. I volunteer for many organizations and do lots of gratis writing for them. Last week I spent three days on a grant. This intellectual exercise required focus, brevity and originality. When I finished the grant I was pleased with the results. My language skills were there, in black and white, on each page.

Writing keeps my life moving forward. If I say I'm a writer I have to keep writing, not sometimes, but all the time. A new book idea is percolating in my mind. I'm excited about the idea and even more excited about the work it demands. I'm so blessed to be a writer!

Reading 12

Recovering From my Daughter's Sudden, Tragic Death

Grieving is hard work. It's really hard for me because I'm grieving for three loved ones at once. All of these deaths were painful, but my daughter's death was the most painful of all. Relatives and friends rallied to help me. Their support lasted for weeks and then it began to fade.

Author Judy Tatelbaum writes about this response in her book, **The Courage to Grieve.** People start to pull back, she explains, "as if the time for grieving were over and we were expected to resume our normal lives . . ." But my life is not normal. Recovering from my daughter's sudden death is the greatest challenge of my life.

Therease A. Rando, PhD, writes about sudden death in her book, **How to go on Living When Someone you Love Dies.** With sudden death there is no chance to say goodbye, notes Rando. "We wish we could have known in order to say and do what we wanted to, we wish we were there for one brief moment with our loved one to tell him we loved him." The last time I saw my daughter she was laughing in the sunshine. I wish I had told her I loved her. Life goes on, however, and I'm working on recovery. How am I doing it?

I cry a lot. Sometimes I know when I'm going to cry and sometimes I don't. "Today was a day of tears," I told my husband. His reply: "Good."

I cut myself some slack. If dinner is lousy, so be it. If the laundry isn't done, so be it. If I miss a meeting, so be it. This is my life and my grief.

I talk about my daughter. When I'm speaking with relatives and friends I include stories about her. Telling these stories keeps my daughter alive in my mind. Her children love hearing the stories, too.

I write about grief. In the last three months I've written a dozen articles about post-death grief. Writing the articles helps me and I hope their content helps others.

I recheck constantly. Are the car keys in my purse? Did I lock the door? Do I have enough money? Rechecks like these help me to avoid mix-ups and assure me that I'm not losing my mind.

I walk for health. Before my daughter died, I walked at least 10,000 steps a day. After she died, I stopped walking. But I have to take care of myself, so I'm back on my walking program. It feels good.

I laugh all I can. My wacky New York humor may be the thing that gets me through grief. Jokes and one-liners are creeping back into my conversation. Laughing with my husband brings me joy. Laughing with my friends makes me feel whole again.

Reading 13

Time is Different When You're Grieving

Nobody can grieve for me, and I'm working hard on recovery. But my grief flares when well-meaning friends say, "Last year was a hard one for you." Last year? It's only been a few months since my daughter died. When friends say this, they're expressing caring and the fact that their lives have moved on. Though my life is moving forward, it's moving forward at a much slower pace.

Time is different when you're grieving.

My daughter was born on the 23rd day of the month and died on the 23rd day of the month. You can understand why I don't like to see that number on the calendar. I think of my daughter hundreds of times a day. Time goes backwards on the 23rd of each month. In my mind I see pictures of my daughter as a baby, toddler, elementary, high school and college student.

Most of all, I think about the things my daughter accomplished in her short life and hope she knew she had "made it."

Time goes backwards when I see the gifts my daughter bought for me. Each one was chosen with care. Some, like an embroidered apron, were made with love. When the twins gave my husband his birthday present, an astronomy book my daughter had bought for him months ago, time went backwards again. His pleasure in the book was clear and so was his grief.

In the middle of the night time often stands still. I awaken from a sound sleep and realize I'm crying. Once I'm awake, I'm awake for several hours. Disjointed thoughts come to mind: memories of our last Christmas together, working together at the church rummage sale, and the talks we shared. Time is passing, yet I feel stuck in time.

Time inches forward again when I'm with the twins. They still come for dinner every Sunday because that's what their mother would have wanted. She started the tradition and my husband and I, and our former son-in-law, continue it. Painful as it is, we tell stories about my daughter and her joy in being a mother.

What will the future bring? Though I can't predict future time, I know these things: I will savor every day of my life, every moment with my husband, and every moment with my grandchildren. The best gift I can give them is the gift of my time. For the hours I spend with my grandchildren will help them remember their mother and the life skills she gave them.

Time is different when you're grieving. Thankfully, healing comes with the passage of time.

Reading 14

Regular Exercise may Help you Cope With Grief

I had been on a walking program for years. After two loved ones died on the same weekend, I walked occasionally. Five months later my brother died and my walking program came to a halt. This was too bad, because exercise has many benefits. Mayo Clinic describes these benefits in a website article, *Depression and Anxiety: Exercise Eases Symptoms*.

According to Mayo, exercise boosts confidence, distracts from anxiety and depression, gets you out and about, and helps you cope. Exercise is also beneficial to mental health. "A growing volume of research shows that exercise can also help improve symptoms of certain medical conditions such as depression and anxiety," the article says.

Even short exercise spurts – just 10-15 minutes – can improve your mood.

Grief expert Therese A. Rando, PhD, talks about exercise in her book, *How to Go on Living When Someone You Love Dies*. Rando thinks exercise helps to reduce the aggressive feelings associated with grief. And Harriet B. Braiker, PhD, author of *Getting Up When You're Feeling Down*, sees a relationship between physical and psychological fitness. We need to schedule activities for both, she says, but shouldn't over-schedule our time. "On the other hand, don't be so easy on yourself that you revert to old habits."

During the early stage of grief, I reverted to the old habit of comfort food. Fortunately, I realized this and changed my diet. But I wasn't aware of my lack of exercise. This is understandable. First, I wasn't sleeping well. Each night I would awaken from sleep, sometimes in tears, and lie awake for hours. Being awake at night made me sleepy during the day. Second, my mind was so filled with details – names, addresses, phone numbers, emails, thank you notes, bank statements, receipts, bills, and probate – I could hardly think.

Exercise was the last thing on my mind. I sat on the couch for hours, remembering, crying and worrying. Television programs diverted my grief for a while and then I'd have a reality check. Grief had turned me into a blob and something had to be done about it.

One morning I got up, clipped my pedometer to my waist, and asked my husband to join me for a walk. Walking is my exercise choice, but you may prefer something else. Don't make the mistake I made. I forgot to do my stretching exercises and had terrible leg cramps. Instead of easing back into my walking program, I walked 9,552 steps the first day. The next morning I had aches and pains in my legs.

These pains are gone now and I'm back on my daily walking program. The pains of grief are also subsiding. I feel better physically, mentally, and the excess pounds are slipping away. When I'm walking, I think about my daughter, father-in-law, and brother. Some memories are unpleasant and painful. Other memories make me laugh and that's good. I'm walking away from grief to a new life.

Reading 15

---∞∞∞---

Grief Recovery: A Process That Demands new Ways of Thinking

I feel like I'm walking through mud. The journey is hard, but I have to keep going, for there is more grief work to do. You understand this work if you're grieving. Grief is a series of processes, according to Therese A. Rando, PhD, author of *How to Go on Living When Someone You love Dies*. Developing a relationship with the deceased is one of these processes.

"You can have an appropriate, sustained, loving and symbolic relationship with the person who has died," she writes.

I understood her point, but was confused by the word relationship, so I looked it up in the dictionary. Relationship is defined as a connection, association, or involvement; connection between persons by blood or marriage; an emotional connection between two people.

But I think of a relationship as interaction. I expect to see my loved one and for that person to see me. I expect to talk to my loved one and for that person to reply. I expect to share news with my loved one and for that person to respond. I expect to make plans with my loved one and for my loved one to help. I expect to spend holidays and birthdays and special days with my loved one.

None of these things will happen.

In order to have a relationship with the deceased "you must have a clear image of him," Rando says, an image that includes positives and negatives. Here's where I ran into trouble. My daughter's childhood was a troubled one, my father-in-law had memory disease (which was getting worse,) and my brother and I were estranged. What could I do?

I read the relationship section of Rando's book again and one sentence stood out. "Part of developing a new relationship with your loved one is learning what you can keep and what you must relinquish now that he is physically dead." As the weeks passed I was able to choose which memories to discard and which ones to keep. I'm still doing this.

Judy Tatelbaum's book, *The Courage to Grieve*, was also helpful to me. As she writes, "We are recovering when we can look at life ahead as worth living." With full recovery, she goes on to say, we're able to look back at the past and know "we have fully grieved and survived the darkest hours." Thankfully, my hours are getting brighter by the day.

Now I'm able to talk about my departed loved ones without bursting into tears. (Occasionally, I relapse.) I can laugh about the experiences we shared. I can find comfort in the happiness my loved ones brought to my life. I can treasure the moments I spend with my husband, my remaining daughter, and my extended family. In other words, I'm creating a new life.

When you create a new life you're creating a new reality. Granger E. Westberg writes about this reality in his book, *Good Grief*. As we struggle to affirm a new reality, "we find that we need not be afraid of the real world," he says. "We can live in it again."

Reading 16

⊸⊶⊷⊸⊶

Honoring Your Loved One's Memory With a Favorite Foods Dinner

My father-in-law died on February 25, 2007. He had been in failing health and had memory disease. When family members learned he had been admitted to the hospital, we knew the end was near. Dad stayed in the hospital for a week and was finally returned to his apartment in Assisted Living for end-of-life care.

Two deaths on one weekend sent shock waves through the family. Though we were overcome with grief, we could only grieve for one person at a time. Of course we cried for Dad, but most of our tears were for a young mother who died too soon. The family decided to have a memorial in honor of Dad at a later date.

How could we honor his life?

Nothing brought Dad more pleasure than having dinner with his family. He often took us out to dinner at his favorite restaurant. Dad was profoundly hard of hearing so they seated us at a corner table when possible. The servers also accommodated to Dad's unusual orders.

One server asked Dad what he wanted and he replied, "Tissues." She returned with a mound of tissues on a tray. Dad used to enjoy thick soups and chowders, but towards the end of his life he wanted broth. Since he had forgotten the word broth Dad ordered "soup without chow," a phrase we had to translate. Minutes later the server would return with a steaming bowl of broth and salty crackers.

Family members thought a Favorite Foods Dinner would be a fitting way to honor Dad's life. We had three requirements for the dinner: 1) easy preparation and clean-up; 2) include some fun; 3) make it meaningful. Six months after Dad's death we had the dinner at my sister and brother-in-law's home.

A large photo of Dad greeted family members when they walked in. For easy clean-up, we used paper plates, napkins and cups. As for dinner, there was hardly a healthy calorie in sight. The menu: Kentucky Fried chicken, mashed potatoes, gravy, coleslaw, smoked oysters on crackers, cheese, fresh fruit (for a few vitamins), chocolate-marshmallow cookies, and ice cream.

I typed a list of Dad's sayings and gave one to each person. Though Dad was no longer with us, his sayings revealed his personality, ethics and humor. Some of them:

- After age 40 you should back up your car as little as possible.
- Take credit for what you do.
- This is going to be the best trip ever!
- Money spent on education is never wasted.
- I don't want to be neatenized.

But I forgot one of Dad's most famous sayings, "When are we going to have fat and salt?" My husband and I had Dad for dinner many times and I cooked nutritious, low-fat meals, a fact that didn't escape his notice. Dad never complained about dinner, but his question was his complaint. Our Favorite Foods Dinner ended with a slide show and the photos of Dad with his family sparked tears and laughter.

Have you lost a loved one? Consider honoring him or her with a Favorite Foods Dinner. Family members would be glad to help you with the arrangements and menu. You may even indulge in fat and salt. Then sit around the table and tell stories of the person you knew and loved so much.

Reading 17

<hr>

Grief Responses: How do you Lose an Egg?

Nobody can grieve for me, I must do it myself, and in my own way. Recovering from loss is hard work and I'm working hard at it. Despite the progress I've made, I'm still forgetful, and the other day I lost an egg. I was going to a lengthy meeting and lunch would be late, so I decided to eat an egg to tide me over.

After I put the skillet on the stove I reached for the egg and it was gone. I searched the counters. No egg. I checked the refrigerator shelves. No egg. I looked for a splat on the floor. No egg. Finally, I looked on the kitchen desk and found the unbroken egg in the mail pile. You may lose an egg and other things if you're grieving. Forgetfulness is a common response to grief and it has four main causes.

There are so many things to do. You need to notify relatives, put a notice in the newspaper, arrange for burial or cremation, plan a memorial service, and keep up with your life. If your loved one died suddenly, you may have some unfinished business. As *Special Challenges for the Survivors of Sudden or Traumatic Death*, an article on the Death and Dying website explains, "The unfinished business may be domestic concerns but can also be work-related or legal matters."

Your mind is constantly diverted by grief. Forgetfulness is an emotional response to grief. I didn't remember where I had put the egg because I had a sudden memory of my daughter. Sometimes I have flashbacks and they are painful. Yet I know I must feel pain in order to recover. Indeed, the recovery road is paved with stones of pain.

The death of a loved one forces you to let go. Letting go is a painful, heart-wrenching process that takes months or even years. Grief Watch, a website for bereaved families and caregivers, notes that "letting go forever to someone you love is a challenge." Though your feelings of sadness lessen, the website continues, you will have times when you miss your loved one and feel sad.

You're constantly playing catch-up. Therese A. Rando, PhD, author of *How to Go on Living When Someone You Love Dies*, thinks the grief process makes us less effective and productive. When you think you're caught up, you fall behind. "For a while it will be impossible for you to function exactly at the same level after a major loss," she writes. Her recommendations: Don't make major decisions too soon, get some support, think through your decisions, and get feedback from those you trust.

Forgetfulness is just one response to grief. You may not lose an egg, but you may do other silly things. These silly things will make you laugh later. Just like grief, laughter is one of the things that make us human.

Reading 18

When Does the Crying Stop?

Surgeons worked all through the night to save my daughter, but they couldn't. Her injures were too severe. After her death and my father-in-law's death, I cried daily for months. Jeffrey A. Kottler details the stages of crying in his book, *The Language of Tears*.

Crying starts slowly, Kottler says, and "gathers momentum, builds in power and force, until it dissipates its energy with a crash, then whimper." He thinks each person feels a release from crying at a different point [in time]. You may be overcome with tears if your loved one just died. When does the crying stop?

The crying stops when you accept the nature of death. Definitions of death and loss are posted on the www.dyingabout.com website. A sudden death occurs within the onset of symptoms. An accidental death, as you might expect, is a random accident. But a traumatic death is violent, random and unpredictable. My daughter's death – blunt force head trauma – was a traumatic one, and I had to accept this fact.

The crying stops when you accept the relationship with your loved one. This relationship may be a loving one, happy, competitive, smooth, unreliable or painful. My daughter's high school years were troubled ones, and it wasn't easy to be her parent. She turned her life around, became a composite engineer, earned an MBA, and was an outstanding mother. I have found comfort in her accomplishments.

The crying stops when you let go. Rabbi Pesach Krauss and Morrie Goldfischer write about crying in their book, *Why Me? Coping With Grief, Loss, and Change*. Parting with a loved one is a wrenching experience, they say, and "there is no easy way to let go." But we must let go in order to move forward with life. Time does heal and, as the days pass, I hope you are able to let go and be grateful for your loved one's life.

The crying stops when you move beyond pain. Grief expert Therese A. Rando, PhD, has written about this. She thinks being able to talk about your loved one without crying is a sign of recovery. As Rando explains, "You lead the pain, it doesn't lead you." Seven months after the multiple losses in our family, I'm able to lead the pain.

The crying stops when you give thanks. My daughter was born on Thanksgiving Day 45 years ago and I'm thankful for her life. I'm also thankful for my twin grandchildren. My father-in-law loved life and lived it to the fullest. I'm thankful for his examples, My brother loved books and I'm not only thankful for his example, I share this love. Golda Meir once said, "Those who do not know how to weep with their whole heart don't know how to laugh either."

I have wept with my whole heart and it is healing.

Reading 19

The Grief and Comfort of Organ Donation

My daughter had signed an organ donor card, but my husband and I didn't know it. We learned of her decision after she was severely injured in the car crash. Doctor after doctor was called in, each one a specialist, and they tried valiantly to save her life. Finally, the supervising surgeons told us our daughter was brain dead. Did we want to proceed with organ donation?

I was already in shock. The thought of donating my daughter's organs was another shock and I was worried sick about my 15-year-old twin grandchildren. They had just lost their mom – their best friend and protector – and we had lost our daughter. The surgeon described the organ harvesting procedure and, though I was an organ donor myself, I didn't want to hear it.

Mayo Clinic discusses organ donation in a website article, *Organ Donation: Don't Let Myths Stand in Your Way*. One myth is that doctors won't work as hard to save the patient's life if he or she is an organ donor. This isn't true, nor is the myth that the patient may still be alive when the organs are harvested. "Even after death, every effort is made to ensure that your loved one's body is treated with the same degree of respect as someone who is alive," the article notes.

My husband and I agreed to organ donation and signed the legal papers. The twins said their last goodbyes to their mom and the images of their sorrow are clear in my mind. Two days later we received a call from the organ donor organization. Our daughter's organs had saved three lives and, thanks to her generosity, two strangers now see. When I heard this news I sobbed uncontrollably.

Weeks later we received a leather-bound certificate from the organ donor organization in recognition of our daughter. The twins received individual certificates and barely glanced at them. I understood their reaction. They didn't want leather-bound certificates, they wanted their mother back and we wanted our daughter.

The grief associated with organ donation is an odd thing. First, it makes the finality of death all too clear. Though it's related to general grief, this kind of grief seems separate. The Grief Link website discusses organ-donor grief in an article, *Grief Reactions Associated With Organ Donation*. According to the article, organ donation may come as a shock to relatives. This was true for my husband and me.

Today, I find a measure of comfort in the fact that my daughter was an organ donor. As the Grief Link article says, "It is an opportunity for something positive to come out of tragedy." My daughter cared about others and this caring continues after her death.

We have received several letters from the organ donor organization. One was about grief and another was an invitation to a gathering of organ donor families, something we're not ready for yet. The hardest day will be my daughter's birthday, which is next week, and I know I'll cry. I also know I'll find comfort in my daughter's generosity – generosity beyond measure.

Reading 20

Having a Happy Birthday After a Loved One has Died

September 27th is my birthday. When my husband left for work, he kissed me and said, "Happy Birthday, Hon." After three deaths in the family, I didn't think I would have a happy day at all.

"I'll try," I replied.

For months I'd been walking around in a fog or thinking about the basics of life. Who was I? What do I do? Could I still do it? Would I be happy again? Daniel Goleman, PhD, discusses the body's responses to happiness in his book, **Emotional Intelligence**. According to him, happiness increases activity "in a brain center that inhibits negative feelings and fosters an increase in available energy, and a quieting of those that generate worrisome thought."

Happiness also gives the body a chance to rest, Goleman says, and generates enthusiasm and energy for pursuing our goals.

I didn't have much energy lately. Three successive deaths had generated hundreds of worrisome thoughts. I wasn't sleeping well. The financial and legal paperwork came in faster than I could process it. Though I made daily "To Do" lists, at the end of the day the lists were longer, not shorter.

Since I had been in crisis before and have good coping skills, I've learned how to care for myself. Kelly Osmont, MSW, writes about self-care in a booklet titled, **More Than Surviving: Caring for Yourself While You Grieve**. "Your life is important," she writes. "To regain a sense of control over your own life, start by taking charge of its direction now."

What an empowering idea! I could take charge of my birthday. Maybe I wouldn't have a "happy birthday" in the ordinary sense of the phrase, but I could have a productive and meaningful one. How did I spend the day? I did some of the things I love most.

Cooking is one of my passions. Fall apples had arrived in the grocery stores. I baked some apple-cinnamon muffins. The smell of the baking muffins was comforting and took me back to childhood. I froze the muffins for another day.

Decorating is another of my passions. We had needed a bedside table in the guest room for years. I ordered a table from a catalog store and paid for it with credit card points. It was almost like getting a table for free. The table will be delivered next week.

Volunteering is also a passion and I volunteer for health organizations. I was working on a nutrition outreach project. This was the perfect day to finalize details and write the press release – tasks that took hours. When my husband returned from work he asked, "How are you?"

"Fine," I said. "I had a productive and meaningful day. I worked on the nutrition project, ordered a bedside table, and baked muffins." My husband wanted to take me out for dinner but I wanted to stay home. We had an easy supper (clam chowder and apple pie) and retired early. I snuggled in my husband's arms, whispered "happy birthday," and went to sleep.

Reading 21

Coping With the Anniversary Reactions
That Come With Grief

Recovering from multiple losses has been heart-wrenching. While I've made progress, I worry about the anniversary reactions that await me. I had an anniversary reaction on my birthday, and it was so painful I dread the holidays. What is an anniversary reaction?

Mayo Clinic defines the term on its website in an article titled, *Grief: Coping With Reminders After a Loss*. An anniversary reaction is a return of strong feelings on special days, according to Mayo Clinic. These reactions can be so strong that the grieving person feels the same way as when their loved one died. "The return of these feelings is not necessarily a setback in the grieving process," notes Mayo.

That was good news and I could certainly use some good news right now.

The US Dept. of Health and Human Services discusses anniversary reactions in a website article, *Anniversary Reactions to a Traumatic Event: The Recovery Process Continues*. Knowing what to expect can be a helpful thing, the article says, and "can provide an opportunity for emotional healing." That was good news, too.

Grief expert Therese A. Rando, PhD, talks about anniversary reactions to holidays in her book, *How to Go on Living When Someone You Love Dies*. Rando thinks anniversary reactions are normal responses to grief and there is no right or wrong way to handle them. "The important thing to remember is that you and your family do have options about how to cope with the holidays," she writes. More good news.

After considering my options, I decided to prepare myself for anniversary reactions. These are the steps I'm taking.

I confront my dread. When this feeling overcomes me, I think about positive memories of my loved ones. My daughter's accomplishments are one of the first things I think about. She set goals, worked to achieve them, achieved them, and then set new goals. What a wonderful role model for her children.

I accept help. My husband and I have been married for 50 years and our love for each other continues to grow. Because we love each other, we take care of each other. This mutual support system, along with the support from family and friends, is helping me to recover.

I focus on positives. "Nobody deserves to go through what you have," a friend said. Yet I have a good life: food, clothing, a car, and a "feel good" house. In addition to a loving husband I have twin grandchildren, a loving family, caring friends, and a writing career.

I'm changing patterns. Our daughter was born on Thanksgiving Day. Family members know the holiday would be difficult for us, so they decided to break the pattern, and dinner will be at a new location. We think this is a great idea and look forward to being with family.

Anniversary reactions are painful, but I wouldn't feel this pain had I not loved my daughter, father-in-law, and brother so much. This love, and the miracle of life, is a blessing.

Reading 22

Staying Busy Makes my Grief Journey Easier

The news of our multiple losses spread quickly. A friend called to express her condolences and tell me something I hadn't known. Her son died when he was only 17 years old. "I understand how you're feeling," she said. "Stay busy. It really helps."

While I appreciated her advice, I also worried about it. I've known people who stayed busy, far too busy, after a loved one died in an attempt to avoid emotional pain. Besides, I'd been studying grief for years, co-authored a book about it, and written articles about it. In order to recover, I knew I had to accept the pain of loss.

Still, I was willing to try the "stay busy" approach. It's working for me and may work for you. How does staying busy help?

Staying busy keeps me from becoming isolated. In an article, *Family Issues and Problems*, published on the Baylor University website, Charles Kemp writes about terminal illness and the problems families face, including isolation. Caregivers have few opportunities for social contact, Kemp says, and they often feel isolated. The same is true of mourning. I refused to get caught in the isolation trap and resumed my volunteer efforts.

Staying busy gives me a break from grief. My husband and I were so overcome with grief we thought we would have to stop working. We didn't do this. Instead, we made a point of returning to work. "Being at work makes me feel better," my husband said. I feel the same way. When I'm writing I'm in a happy world.

Staying busy makes time pass quickly. Michael Creagan, MD, a Mayo Clinic oncologist, writes about time in his article, *Grief: A Mayo Clinic Doctor Confronts Painful Emotions*. According to Creagan, "Time does have the ability to make the acute, searing pain of loss less intense." But time does not cure, he goes on to say, and the feelings of loss and emptiness may never go away. Though I will always miss my loved ones, I was blessed to have them in my life.

Staying busy helps my mind process grief. The human mind is probably the ultimate computer. When I'm busy my mind is sorting data, retrieving data, reviewing images, problem-solving and, most important, processing grief. Though I think about my loved ones, when I'm busy the pain is not as acute.

Staying busy is helping me forge a new life. At first, I set one goal a day. Several weeks later I set two goals. Today, nine months after our family tragedies, I set even more. For I've learned that when I'm not busy my recovery goes backwards. Grief is a personal journey and if you're grieving now you may want to try the "stay busy" approach.

This approach doesn't mean we've forgotten our loved ones. We still miss them, still cry, and still love them. Our loved ones would want us to do things that make us happy, try new things, and enjoy every moment of life. Let's do that for ourselves and for them.

Reading 23

❖❖

When you Read the Sympathy Cards Again and Cry

Every time I walked by the box, I flinched. It held the hundreds of sympathy cards we've received after three deaths in the family. I didn't want to look at the box, let alone open it. A widowed friend asked me if I had re-read the cards. "No," I sighed. "I just can't do it."

Re-reading the cards would open up grief wounds and my friend understood this. "The day will come when you read the cards again and cry," she said, "and you will find new comfort in them." That day was yesterday.

I recognized most of the names on the cards, but there were some I didn't recognize. However, I was aware of the caring that the cards represented. One read, "Sometimes the hurt is too big for words," a sentence I understood very well. I was often at a loss for words to describe my grief. In fact, grief had slowed my mind's ability to retrieve vocabulary words.

The box held cards from my daughter's co-workers. My daughter, a composite engineer with an MBA degree, had managed three production lines at an engine manufacturing plant. A group card made me cry, especially the note from one co-worker that said he was glad my daughter had been his manager.

I'm glad I read the cards again because I found a memorial check in one and cash in another. Gathering the courage to re-read the cards took me nine months. This time frame is part of my grief "fingerprint." Andrea Gambill describes these fingerprints in an article with the same name, published in the October 2007 issue of *Grief Digest*. "You have the right to be an individual," Gambill says, "to be different in some ways from every other griever."

If you're grieving, you have received sympathy cards. The cards tell you that people care but, like me, you may not want to read them again. Should you do it? Yes, but only when you feel the time is right. As my friend predicted, I found new comfort in the cards. The cards represented the thoughts and prayers of hundreds of people and I could feel their support.

I was really touched by the handmade cards. One was from an artist friend and another was from a cousin who is an expert photographer. A hand-lettered card with a quote from Thoreau touched my soul. The quote: "Every blade in the field, every leaf in the forest, lays down its life in its season, as beautifully as it was taken up."

Bettyclare Moffatt, in her book, *Soulwork: Clearing the Mind, Opening the Heart, Replenishing the Spirit*, lists 12 directions we may take for soul work living. Direction number 10 spoke to me and it says, in part, "Be willing to learn, to grow, to start over." Sympathy cards have helped me do this and I'm creating a new life. The day will come when you read the cards again and draw comfort from them.

Reading 24

⊷⊷⊶⊶

Multiple Losses Throw off the Stages and Timing of Grief

I'm familiar with the stages of grief – denial, anger, bargaining, depression, and acceptance – and have thought about them a lot after three loved ones died in succession. As time passed, I became aware of two things. Moving on to the next stage didn't stop me from going backwards to previous ones.

This week I'm back to denial, and can hardly believe my loved ones are gone. I don't know if the approaching holidays caused this, but I know denial is unsettling. When I think about the Sunday dinners I enjoyed with my daughter and twin grandchildren I'm overcome with grief. After dinner we swapped stories and jokes, and I can almost see my daughter sitting in the wing-back chair across from me, laughing and slapping her knees.

Most of my grief thoughts are about my daughter because she was only 45 years old when she died, whereas my father-in-law was 98½ years old. I missed my father-in-law, but had never really grieved for him. One morning I awakened with thoughts of Dad and spent the entire day sobbing for the loss of this wonderful man. I cried for him on other days as well.

Finally, I realized I was grieving for my loved ones singly and in the order they died. You may be grieving the same way if you have experienced multiple losses. I think multiple losses throw off the stages and timing of grief. What's more, I have no idea of how long my grief journey will last.

The Victoria Hospice in British Columbia has published a booklet about multiple losses titled, **Difficult Grief and Multiple Losses.** As the booklet points out, dealing with multiple losses takes time and energy. "People around you find it hard to comprehend the extent of your grief or to tolerate the intensity of your feelings," it says.

I've found this all too true. Friends gasp when they see me in the grocery store and one turned her cart around. Similar things may have happened to you. Our friends aren't unkind, they just don't know what to say because our losses are so huge. Instead of worrying about friends' responses we need to ask ourselves, "How can we heal?"

Victoria Hospice offers some helpful suggestions in its booklet. They include finding new support people, being aware of grief themes, pacing ourselves, connecting with others, regular prayer and meditation, and dealing with one thing at a time. I've found it helpful to deal with one loss at a time.

Bob Deits, MTh writes about timing in his book, **Life After Loss: A Practical Guide to Renewing Your Life After Experiencing Major Loss.** Six months after a loss you feel better, Deits explains, and then something spoils your mood. You hear a familiar song or see someone who looks like your deceased loved one. "Whatever it is, your response is to have the roof cave in" on your emotions and your day.

This is scary and we may think we're starting grief all over again. But Deits considers these experiences as "signs of forward movement." I've marked off many mileposts since my loved ones died. You have also marked off mileposts if you're grieving for one loss or many. Each one is a step forward to a new life.

Reading 25

Another Death: How Much can a Family Take?

I thought I knew a lot about grief and never thought, even for a second, that life had more to teach me. Last week my former son-in-law, the father of my twin grandchildren, died in a car crash. I can hardly believe he died the same way my daughter died.

When I heard about the fourth death in the family, my mind zapped back to the first stage of grief – shock and disbelief. I was overcome with grief and sobbed for my daughter, father-in-law, brother, former son-in-law, my grandkids, and myself. Then I stopped sobbing. In fact, my mind raced forward to the final stage of grief, acceptance.

Judith R. Bernstein, PhD, writes about the stages of grief in her book. **When a Bough Breaks.** Many researchers believe the stages of grief that Dr. Elisabeth Kubler-Ross identified, she notes, but "all agree that these stages are completely flexible and there is no such thing as orderly progression." I understood her point, indeed, I lived it.

To go from disbelief to acceptance was amazing. I may never fully understand the process, but I think it happened because I've studied grief, have the experience that comes with age, and have good coping skills. One coping skill is sticking to a routine as much as possible.

I'm trying to get my grandkids to stick to their routine. We had planned to have Thanksgiving dinner with the extended family and the kids wanted to do this. Twenty-three family members gathered around various tables, and I saw them "close ranks" to help the kids. But the kids wonder, friends wonder, and we wonder why both of their parents died.

As I've done before, I turned to Rabbi Harold Kushner's book, **When Bad Things Happen to Good People**. Nobody knows why four of our family members died in nine months, but if you believe Rabbi Kushner, bad things happen randomly. "They do not happen for any good reason which would cause us to accept them willingly," he writes. "But we can give them a meaning."

I'm giving new meaning to my life by caring for my grandkids. This care includes healthy meals, clean laundry, shopping service, shuttle service, attending concerts and sports events, and listening. When my grandkids share their thoughts with me I listen as though their lives depend on each word.

I'm giving new meaning to my life by writing about my losses. One of the reasons writers do what they do is to gain understanding. I thought I was writing about multiple losses to recover. Now I realize that I'm writing about multiple losses to survive.

If you have suffered a loss I hope you give new meaning to your life. Like me, you may find meaning in caring for children. Donating to a religious community or health organization may also give your life new meaning. This moment in time – my grandkids' high school and college years – will define my life. I will care for my grandkids until I take my last breath. Despite the pain of multiple losses, I feel blessed. Multiple losses have taught me that every moment of life is precious and I won't waste a single one.

Reading 26

⋘⊙⋙

Writing Your way Through Grief

My mind is so cluttered I can hardly think. Maybe I'm sleep-deprived. Our 15-year-old grandkids live with us now, and my husband and I get up at 5:15 a.m. to feed them breakfast and drive them to school We pick up the kids after school and start the shuttle service to gymnastics, meetings, ski club, track, band concerts and other events.

I had been writing articles about my grief for the Internet and found the process extremely helpful. Could I still find time to write? The only way to find out was to experiment.

Writing in the early afternoon didn't work because I had to pick up the kids at school. Late afternoon writing didn't work because I had to fix dinner and shuttle the kids to activities. Early morning was the only time left, and it works. As soon as the twins leave for school, I start the laundry. Then I go downstairs to the office and write. I learn things when I write and also discover new things about myself.

According to Bob Bittner, President of the American Society of Journalists and Authors (ASJA), non-writers fail to grasp an important fact. "Many of us [writers] don't write to change others' lives," he says. "We write to change ourselves." Bittner makes this observation in his article, **You Should Write a Book**, published in the December 2007 issue of the ASJA newsletter.

You don't have to be a professional writer to write your way through grief.

Kathleen Adams, LPC, RPT, talks about documenting grief in her article, *Managing Grief Through Journal Writing*, published in the January 2001 issue of MADDavocate, which is put out by Mothers Against Drunk Driving. Her article contains a dozen tips for journal writing, including listing three words that describe your feelings each day.

While I understand the logic behind Adams' idea, I couldn't follow it due to the stress of multiple losses. If I thought of one descriptive word, I was doing well. Today, that word is overwhelmed. Maybe you're feeling overwhelmed too, so overwhelmed you can't find the time or energy to write.

Believe me, I understand. Still, I hope you will document your grief in words because it will help you. From my perspective as a professional writer, not to write was to give up on life. I couldn't do that and you shouldn't either. Each piece we write, whether it is long, short, or just a few words, is a marker on our grief journey. These markers lead us to new feelings, discoveries and wisdom.

So get out a pen, or boot up the computer, and write your way through grief. There is a new life ahead of us, and writing helps us to prepare for it. When you write your way through grief, you find your way through grief.

Reading 27

Teens in the House Again: A Grandparent's Blessing

Now that our grandkids live with us the house is filled with teenage sounds: beeping alarm clocks, guitar chords, rock music, running feet and occasional laughter. (We hope to hear more laughter soon.) The four of us are trying to get along. While we disagree on some things, I think we agree on one – grief stinks.

Grief Stinks is a chapter title in Lynne B. Hughs' book, ***You are Not Alone: Teens Talk About Life and the Loss of a Parent***. Hughs lost both parents at an early age and understands kids' grief. She founded Comfort Zone Camp for grieving kids and thinks talking about happier times helps teens cope with grief.

Though I often talk about happier times, inside I'm still grieving for my loved ones. Staying upbeat for the kids is a challenge. I have smiled when I wanted to weep. I have comforted when I needed comfort. I have kept quiet when I wanted to shout. As Lynne Hughs observes, "Sometimes you have to walk through that 'wall of pain' to get to the other side of healing."

Yet having teens in the house is helping me to heal. How has my life changed?

I'm learning new things. My grandson is a computer whiz and I'm learning about wireless networks, gigabytes and thumb drives. My granddaughter is on the gymnastics team and I'm learning about "burns," pointed toes, and graceful dismounts.

I'm moving constantly. After four deaths in the family I pigged out on comfort food and gained five pounds. I thought about joining the health club again, but didn't get around to it. Forget the health club. I'm up at 5:15 a.m. and don't stop moving until my head hits the pillow at night. The extra pounds are gone.

I'm laughing again. When I called the twins for supper the other night, my granddaughter called, "Coming." But my grandson didn't reply and I asked his sister to find him. She emailed her brother and, within seconds, he was sitting at the table.

I'm planning a future. Eight years ago we took our family to the Isle of Man, the birthplace of the Hodgson clan. It's a fairy tale island in the middle of the Irish Sea. If air fares drop, their high school graduation present will be another trip to the Isle.

I'm feeling younger. I look my age and, while I'm not young in years, I'm young in spirit. Bob Deits discusses the importance of attitude in his book, ***Life After Loss: The A Practical Guide to Renewing Your Life After Experiencing Major Loss***. Deits asks readers two questions: 1) How old are you? 2) Do you think of yourself as old?

"Personally, some days I feel quite young, whereas on other days I feel older than dirt," Deits admits. Multiple losses made me feel older than dirt. Indeed, I felt like I was mired in the muck of grief. No more. I'm blessed to have teens in the house again.

Reading 28

⊰⊱

Answering the Question, "How are You?"

Though I've learned to live with multiple losses, they will always be part of my life. Charles M. Meyer, MD, Editor in Chief of *Minnesota Medicine*, makes this point in his editorial, *Living with Loss,* published in the October 2006 issue of the journal. "The time comes when you think grief is gone," Meyer observes, "and then it rises like a phoenix from the ashes and captures you."

"It [grief] never quite leaves you alone."

There is something else that doesn't leave you alone and it's the question, "How are you doing?" If you are grieving you know this, and have been asked the question dozens, even hundreds, of times. It's impossible to answer the question in the early stages of grief. Answering the question takes time.

Judith R. Bernstein, PhD, discusses time in her book, *When a Bough Breaks: Forever After the Death of a Son or Daughter.* "Just as you can't teach a child to walk before his muscles are ready," she writes, "you can't force the mending to proceed before the mourner is ready." I couldn't agree with her more.

Bob Deits discusses the careless things people say in his book, *Life After Loss: A Practical Guide to Renewing Your Life After Experiencing Major Loss.* He thinks people want to hear only one response to "How are you?' As Deits notes, "You will discover very quickly that the only acceptable answer is 'fine,' regardless of how miserable you are feeling at the moment."

So in self-defense I came up with a list of answers to "How are you?"
1. "Fine." I used this reply in the early stages of grief. Of course I wanted to say I felt awful, but I didn't, I said, "fine." Besides, "fine" made it easy for people to bypass an uncomfortable conversation about death, grief and mourning.
2. "Okay." This is a one-word-fits-all-situations answer. When I said "okay," people looked relieved. I thought "okay" was a pretty good answer because it sounded like I was holding my own.
3. "Getting along." I used this reply in the middle stage of grief. The word "along" implies progress and that is encouraging. In truth, I was getting along and moving forward with life.
4. "I'm coping." Only true friends hear this answer, because it leads to in-depth conversation. I have shared my thoughts with people I hardly know, but prefer to share them with close friends. My friends know me well enough to provide feedback.
5. "I'm good." This is my current reply. "Your voice sounds so much better," a friend commented. She is right. I sound better, look better and feel better. Indeed, I'm living a new life.

Four deaths in nine months created a mountain of grief work. I have climbed that mountain. And though I have more grief work to do, I have crossed the boundary between sorrow and joy, and each day is brighter. Now I don't mind if someone asks, "How are you?" I answer, smile, and continue on my way.

Reading 29

⎯⟨⋈⟩⎯

New Year, New Life, New Me

The first anniversary of my daughter's death, February 23rd, was a day I dreaded. Would I fall apart or hold myself together? Would the graveside ceremony help my grandchildren heal? Would spending time with family help them see a future?

I survived a year of tragedy with help from family members. My husband and I are blessed to have a loving and supportive family. Dr. Robert Veniga discusses family support in his book, *A Gift of Hope: How We Survive our Tragedies*. In a healthy family nobody plays the role of martyr, according to Veninga, and nobody is confrontive, self-righteous or accusing.

Instead, family members come together to problem-solve. "When family members roll up their sleeves and diligently search for solutions, the clouds begin to recede," writes Veninga. Many dark, roiling clouds have receded since that terrible weekend a year ago. It was time to celebrate our loved ones' lives.

We decided to hold a short, graveside ceremony, followed by lunch at a local restaurant. Family members gathered around the gravesite at 11:30 a.m. Though we had no plans for what would occur there, an hour before the ceremony I sat at the computer and typed a list titled, "Helen's Legacy." I kept the list short because I wanted my grandkids to remember it.

- Believe in a Higher Power
- Live your beliefs.
- Stay on the AA path.
- Family comes first.
- Love and enjoy your children.
- Get an education and keep learning.
- Find an occupation that doesn't seem like work.
- Share with others even if you have little to give.
- Know what's important and what isn't.
- Help others.
- Laugh every day.

I gave each family member a copy of the list and made some comments. "The first anniversary of Pampa's death is on Monday," I noted. "So I want us to remember him, too. He was one of the finest people I've ever known."

My husband reflected on how much our daughter loved her job, and the promising future that awaited her. Our remaining daughter told a funny story about her sister re-attaching a hunk of fur to the twin's pet hamster with super glue. Everyone laughed. "It worked," my grandson added.

We hugged each other, shed a few tears, and went to the restaurant. Ten of us gathered around the table and everyone was in a good mood. Many things had changed in the last year, including me. While I have the same personality, talents, and interests, I am very different.

Grief has made me stronger. This strength surprises me and I'm also surprised by how often I draw from it. I'm using this strength to protect and raise my grandchildren. "Your grandchildren are keeping you young," my friends say, and they may be right. My husband and I are blessed to have each other and our lives are still an adventure.

Reading 30

—◁⊗▷—

Remembering Your Loved one with a Memory Cook Book

After the death of a loved one, some families make quilts from their loved one's clothes. Other families compile memory books. I did something different for my family; I made a memory cook book. After my mother-in-law died, my sister-in-law and I looked through her old recipe boxes.

We found hand-written recipes, lots of newspaper and magazine clippings, and many duplicates. We threw out the duplicate recipes and saved family favorites, recipes that grandchildren and great grandchildren would enjoy. Reading the recipes brought back memories of family picnics, holiday dinners and snacks Nana prepared for her three growing boys.

I typed the recipes (one per page) and compiled them in a three-ring notebook. The title of the book: ***Favorite Recipes From Nana's Recipe Boxes***. For the cover, I used holiday stationery with a candy-cane border. Each cover had a photo of Nana on it. To protect the recipes from splatters and drips, I put them in plastic notebook sleeves. There were only 25 recipes so I didn't index them. However, I did write a short introduction, and it contained a story that is still clear in my mind.

Nana served Sunday dinner at one p.m. After one dinner, she announced that supper would be cake and ice cream. I laughed because I thought Nana was kidding. But Nana (the only person I've ever known who ate cold butter rolled in sugar) had a sweet tooth and supper was just as advertised. We had huge bowls of French vanilla ice cream and hefty slices of yellow cake with Penuche frosting. What a memory.

Because the cook book was a glimpse of family history, I typed the recipes as Nana wrote them, including abbreviations such as "refrig" for refrigerator, and references to family members and friends. I put the pages in notebooks, tucked rubber spatulas inside, wrapped them, and tied measuring spoons to each one.

So much love had gone into the cook books that I could hardly wait to give them to family members on Christmas morning. A few fancy gifts were exchanged, but my homemade gifts were the hit of the day. Family members told Nana stories as they paged through their cook books.

If you're looking for a meaningful way to remember a loved one, think about compiling a memory cook book. Your cook book will spark stories about the meals you've shared and link the older generation with the younger. Now you're probably wondering about the recipes. My favorite recipe is the one for fudge. Though I don't make fudge, I love the ending. Here is the recipe, just as Nana wrote it so many years ago.

Nana's Fudge 1920

2 c. sugar	¾ c. milk	2 sq. chocolate	½ t. salt
1 T. butter	1 t (teaspoon) vanilla	Nuts	

Mix and cook all ingredients except vanilla & nuts. When it boils up once, lower the heat to a slow boil. After 5 min. begin testing for the softball stage (1/2 tsp. fudge in a saucer of ice water.)

When you can pick up a soft ball in 3 fingers it's ready. Cook it 1 minute more. Remove from stove and cool completely before stirring. Add vanilla and nuts and beat until it looks [like] it's glass and begins to set. Pour into a small, square cake pan. Cut when hard. (If it gets too hard add a few drops of cream at the end of beating.) Cut, enjoy.

Save some for Mother and Dad. Be a good scout and clean up the kitchen afterwards.

Proactive Steps in This Book

Grief takes away your sense of control. Regaining control over your life will take years. There is lots of grief work to do, and it is painful. You must grieve for your losses, come to terms with the past, grapple with the present, keep up with daily chores, take care of others, take care of yourself, re-think values and priorities and plan your future.

How will you get all of this done? Taking proactive steps will lift your spirits and get you on the recovery road. But identifying these steps can be difficult when you're grieving, especially when you're just trying to survive each day. You already have too much responsibility, and proactive steps add more. What a bummer.

As Judith Viorst explains in her book, **Necessary Losses**, "It becomes increasingly clear that the person in charge of us is . . . us, and we may resent the responsibility." Though I had some resentful feelings, I didn't waste time or energy on them. I put most of my energy into proactive steps, and I'm glad I did. If you take proactive steps, I think you will be glad, too.

There are dozens of proactive steps in this anthology and you've read them all. You may be so stressed, however, that you may not remember the steps, so I have summarized them here. Please think of these steps as prompts – actions that focus your mind and lead to solutions. My proactive steps are examples and, while you may take some of them, you will have to find steps that work for you.

Just like baby steps, your first steps will be wobbly and unsure. Will I fall down? What if I hurt myself? Where am I going? Don't worry. Proactive steps are seeds of hope. As you nurture them, the seeds will burst open, push through the darkness, and grow towards the sun. Your grief may become a renewal of growth and life.

Summary of Proactive Steps

- Learn about grief, bereavement, and mourning.
- Write about your grief.
- Write regularly.
- Let yourself cry.
- Find comfort in friends.
- Find comfort in tasks.
- See the spirit behind the things people say.
- Get help if you need it.
- Stay connected to your work.
- Be emotionally kind to yourself.
- Accept the pain of grief.
- Try to lead the pain, instead of the pain leading you.
- Use your support system.
- Re-check your support system now and then.
- Take care of your physical and mental health.
- Laugh all you can.
- Make quiet time part of each day.
- Watch one television newscast a day and no more.
- Pass along the miracles of kindness.
- Conduct occasional reality checks.
- Draw upon your religious and spiritual beliefs.
- Keep family traditions.
- Create new traditions.
- Set new goals.
- Talk about your deceased loved ones.

- Honor your loved ones in thoughtful ways.
- Stick to a routine.
- Stay busy, but not too busy.
- Prepare for anniversary reactions.
- Let go of your deceased loved ones gradually.
- Look for recovery mileposts, such as the return of humor, a cheerful voice, and new social contacts.
- Learn from your grief journey.
- Make something good from grief.
- Be thankful for the gift of life.
- Celebrate life every chance you get.

Words of Hope

My writing project is ending and yours is beginning. Expressing your grief in words is a journey of its own. On this journey I learned about the goodness of others and the resilience of the human spirit. This has been the most challenging year of my life, and I didn't think I would survive it. I discovered I was stronger than I thought.

You will discover many things as you write to recover. If your grief journey is anything like mine, the writing process will steer you toward hope and, with the passage of time, a new life.

Earlier, I said I would end this book on the first anniversary of my daughter's death. This would be a good stopping place and I wanted to explore new writing projects. "What will your next book be about?" my husband asked. During our 50 years of marriage he has asked me this question many times. His question makes me nervous because I can't answer it.

What do I say? "I may never write another book," a reply that makes my husband chuckle. He knows I'll keep writing and I do, too. I just don't know what I will write about. Perhaps I'll write about the eighteenth month and second-year responses to bereavement. Author Bob Deits describes these responses in his book, *Life After Loss: A Practical Guide to Renewing Your Life After Experiencing a Major Loss.*

According to Deits, "Many people meet the anniversary date with a mixture of sadness and hope." He thinks the eighteenth month after the death of a loved one is significant because you've accomplished the impossible. You survived. But sadness returns at this time and it can be so painful you feel like you're starting your grief journey all over again. Fortunately, Deits says this sadness doesn't last long and he considers it a "bump in the road to recovery."

By the second year anniversary, people are starting to move beyond loss and enjoy their lives. Many people feel guilty about their enjoyment, Deits notes. I don't think this will happen to me. My grandchildren have tugged me, at times yanked me, into a new life. Seeing life through their eyes and sharing it with them has revitalized my spirit.

Vamik D. Volkan, MD and Elizabeth Zintl write about the human spirit in their book, *Life After Loss: The Lessons of Grief.* Some people manage to grieve effectively, they point out, while others don't. What's the difference? "The right developmental push – the birth of a child, a new and fulfilling love, a wise therapist – is sometimes all that is needed to help us discover the resources to manage conflict and overcome the likely complication of mourning."

Writing to Recover was my developmental push and it may be yours. I felt the push when I wrote about my humor returning. With each passing month this spark of humor became brighter, and I saw it as a sign of recovery. While I'm amazed at my recovery, I know it is the result of self-examination and grief work. Life feels good again.

This thought led me to Dr. Robert Veniga's book, *A Gift of Hope*. I love this book and turn to it in times of crisis. According to Veniga, we need to take care of our physical and mental health, or as he puts it, "You need to exercise the brain." Writing about your grief journey is brain exercise, an exercise that forces you to retrieve words from memory, learn new words and remember them.

Words rattle around in my head when I'm writing and awaken me at night. Songs also rattle around in my head. I took voice lessons in my high school years and music has always been part of my identity. I belonged to the school choir, church choir, sang solos in church, was a wedding soloist, and part of a traveling show troupe. The last few weeks I've been humming Amazing Grace.

The words of this beloved hymn were written by Rev. John Newton. While the origin of the music is unclear, many think it is an early American folk melody. The simple words and melody touch my soul, especially the line, "I once was lost but now am found." For months, I had been lost in the darkness of grief. Now I have found a new and brighter life.

You may not be musical, but you still have words, words that tell who you are, where you came from, what you are facing, how you are coping, where you are headed, and your struggle to survive. Words are powerful and, as the days pass, I hope your writing empowers you. Writer and reader part here, yet we will always be linked by the loss and grief we share. So I send you virtual hugs and sincere wishes for a good life – a life filled with love, laughter and newfound joy.

Grief Support

Street addresses, phone numbers, e-mail addresses and Website addresses often change. Please re-check these addresses before using them. Contact your faith community and social services for additional support. Your newspaper may also list support groups.

American Association of Pastoral Counselors
9504A Lee Highway
Fairfax, VA 22031-2303
Website http://www.aapc.org
E-mail info@aapc.org

AARP Grief and Loss Programs
601 E Street NW
Washington, DC 20049
Phone 202-434-2260
Toll Free 866-797-2277
Website http://ww.griefandloss.org
E-mail griefandloss@aarp.org

American Hospice Foundation
2120 L Street NW, Suite 200
Washington, DC 20037
Phone 202-223-0204
Toll Free 800-347-1413
E-mail ahf@americanhospice.org

Association for Death Education and Counseling
60 Revere Drive, Suite 500
Northbrook, IL 60062
Phone 847-509-0403
Website http://www.adec.org

American Psychiatric Association
1400 K Street NW
Washington, DC 20005
Phone 888-357-7924
Website www.psych.org
E-mail apaa@psych.org

American Psychological Association
750 First Street NE
Washington, DC 20002-4242
Phone 202-336-5500
Toll Free 800-374-2721

Center for Grief Recovery
1263 West Lyola Ave.
Chicago, IL 60026
Phone 773-274-4600
E-mail information@griefcounrselor.org

GriefNet (an on-line support community)
Website http://www.griefnet.org

Growth House, Inc. (forum about self-help and recovery)
Website http://www.growthhouse.org

Open to Hope Foundation (online resource center) www.opentohope.com

RENEW: Center for Personal Recovery
P.O. Box 125
Berea, KY 40403
Phone 859-986-7878
Website http://www.renew.net

The Compassionate Friends (national office)
P.O. Box 3696
Oak Brook, IL 60522-3696
Phone 630-990-0010
Toll Free 877-969-0010
Website
http://www.compassionatefriends.org

The Grief Blog (interactive forum supervised by a mother-daughter team of psychiatrists) www.thegriefblog.com

Resources

Adams, Kathleen, LPC, RPT. *Managing Grief Through Journal Writing,* The Center for Journal Therapy website www.journaltherapy.com

Baldwin, Christina. *One to One: Self-Understanding Through Journal Writing.* New York: M. Evans and Company, Inc., 1991, p. 6-8.

Bernstein, Judith R., Ph.D. *When a Bough Breaks: Forever After the Death of a Son or Daughter.* Kansas City: Andrews McMeel Publishing, 1998, p. 7-8.

Bittner, Bob. *You Should Write a Book*, "The ASJA Monthly," American Society of Journalists and Authors, Inc. newsletter, December 2007, volume 56, p. 3.

Creagan, Michael, MD. *Grief: A Mayo Clinic Doctor Confronts Painful Emotions*, Mayo Clinic website: www.mayoclinic.com

Death and Dying website. *Special Challenges for Survivors of Sudden or Traumatic Death,* www.death-dyng.com

Deits, Bob, M.Th. *Life After Loss: A Practical Guide to Renewing Your Life After Experiencing Major Loss.* Cambridge, MA: Lifelong Books (Perseus Books Group), 2004, p. 80, 172-176, 191.

Fitzgerald, Helen, PhD. *Helping Yourself Through Grief*, American Hospice Foundation website: www.americanhospice.org

Fitzgerald, Helen. *The Grieving Teen,* American Hospice Foundation website: www.americanhospice.org

Gambill, Andrea. *Fingerprints*, *Grief Digest,* October 2007, p. 2-3.

Goleman, Daniel, PhD. *Emotional Intelligence: Why it Can Matter More than IQ.* New York: Bantam Books, 1997, p. 138-139, 240.

Grief Reactions Associated With Organ Donation, Grief Link website: www.grieflink.com

Hamblen, Jessica, PhD, Friedman, Mark, MD, Schnurr, Paula. *Fact Sheet*

About Anniversary Reactions. US Dept. of Veterans Affairs website: www.va.gov

Hughs, Lynne B. *You Are Not Alone: Teens Talk About Life After the Loss of a Parent.* New York: Scholastic Press, 2005, p. 22, 43.

Kemp, Charles. *Family Issues and Problems,* Baylor University website: www3.baylor.edu/ ~ Charles_Kemp/terminal%20illness/Terminal_Illness. htm

Kushner, Rabbi Harold S. *When Bad Things Happen to Good People,* New York: Avon Books, 1981, p. 46, 136, 148.

Lende, Heather. *If You Lived Here, I'd Know Your Name.* New York: Workman Publishing, 2005, p. 281.

Kottler, Jeffrey A. *The Language of Tears.* San Francisco: Jossey-Bass Publishers, 1996, p. 30-134, 169, 175.

Krauss, Pesach and Goldfischer, Morrie. *Why Me? Coping with Grief, Loss, and Change.* New York: Bantam Books, 1990, p. 54-55, 130.

Mayo Clinic. *Grief: Coping With Reminders After Loss,* Mayo Clinic website, www.mayoclinic.com

Mayo Clinic. *Depression and Anxiety: Exercise Eases Symptoms,* Mayo Clinic website: www.mayoclinic.com

Mayo Clinic. *Organ Donation: Don't Let Myths Stand in Your Way,* Mayo Clinic website: www.mayoclinic.com

Meyer, Charles R., MD. *Living with Loss, Minnesota Medicine,* October 2006, p. 4.

Moffatt, Bettyclare. *Soulwork: Clearing the Mind, Opening the Heart, Replenishing the Spirit.* Berkeley, CA: Wildcat Canyon Press, 1994, p. 25-27, 143, 180.

No author. *Dealing with Sudden, Accidental or Traumatic Death, Journey of Hearts* website: www.journeyofhearts.org/grief/accident2. html

Oliver, Mary. *Thirst, In the Storm.* Boston: Beacon Press, 2006, p. 62-63.

Osmont, Kelly, MSW. *More Than Surviving: Caring for Yourself While You Grieve.* Omaha: The Centering Corporation, 1990, p. 5.

Peck, Peggy. *Grief Following Death in the Family Ebbs in Six Months.* Psychiatric Times website: www.psychiatrictimes.com

Rando, Therese A., Ph.D. *How to Go on Living When Someone You Love Dies.* New York: Lexington Books, 1988, p. 39, 56, 92, 164, 233-236, 284, 289.

Schuett, Dawn. *Death Prompts Intersection Change*, Post-Bulletin, December 21, 2007, p. 1B.

Tatelbaum, Judy, Ph.D. *The Courage to Grieve: Creative Living, Recovery, & Growth Through Grief.* New York: Harper& Rowe, 1980, p. 9, 43, 87, 94, 139.

US Dept. of Health and Human Services, National Mental Health Information Center, *Anniversary Reactions to a Traumatic Event: The Recovery Process Continues,* www.nmicstore.samhsa.gov/topics/pubs.aspx?id = 181&topic = Disaster % 2fTrauma

Veninga, Robert, MD. *A Gift of Hope: How We Survive Our Tragedies.* Boston: Little, Brown and Company, 1985, p. 109, 139-140, 210.

Viorst, Judith. *Necessary Losses: The Loves, Illusions, Dependencies and Impossible Expectations That All of Us Have to Give Up in Order to Grow.* New York: Ballantine Books, 1986, p. 153.

Victoria Hospice Bereavement Program, Victoria, BC. *Difficult Grief and Multiple Losses*, reprinted on the Capital Health website: www.cdha.nshealth.ca/patientinformation/nshealthnet/0982.pdf

Volkan, Vamik, MD and Zintl, Elizabeth. *Life After Loss: The Lessons of Grief.* New York: Macmillan Publishing Company, 1993, p. 31-32, 37, 39, 60.

Westberg, Granger E. Good Grief. Philadelphia: Fortress Press, 1962, p. 64.

Wesley Medical Center. *Donation – The Gift of Life.* Wesley Medical Center website: www.wesleymc.com

Wolfelt, Dr. Alan. National Institute of Mental Health (NIMH) website, www.nimh.nih.gov

Ziccarello, Roe. *10 Grief Steps,* Sound Feelings website: www.soundfeelings.com

Index

Notes

Notes

CENTERING CORPORATION
AND GRIEF DIGEST MAGAZINE
GRIEF RESOURCES

Grief Digest Magazine
1-866-218-0101 • www.centering.org

About the Author

Harriet Hodgson has been an independent journalist for 30 years. She is a member of the Association for Death Education and Counseling and the Association of Health Care Journalists. A prolific writer, Hodgson is the author of 26 books and hundreds of newspaper, newsletter, and Internet articles.

Hodgson's writing comes from experience and she has shared her experiences on more than 150 radio talk shows, including CBS Radio, WCCO Radio, and "Coping With Caregiving," an Internet-only radio program broadcast worldwide. She has appeared on dozens of television stations/programs, including CNN. A popular speaker, Hodgson has given presentations at Alzheimer's, hospice, and public health conferences.

Her work is cited in *Something About the Author, Who's Who of American Women, Who's Who in America,* and *Contemporary Authors*. Hodgson lives in Rochester, Minnesota with her husband, John, and her twin grandchildren. Please log onto www.harriethodgson.com for more information on this busy author and grandmother.

www.centering.org